BEACON

vegetables **organic**
planting

Get out and

propagation
containers garden
lawns mulches

Franck Chauvet
Hélène Lanscotte

CASSELL&CO

Discover...

that 52% of the British population have access to a garden, balcony or roof terrace. ▶ 90

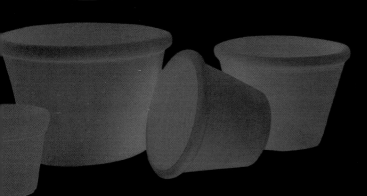

Gardens of philosophy were invented by the Ancient Greeks. Roman gardens were both practical and beautiful. The garden was an integral part of Roman life. It was conceived as a place of physical delight. Through ingenious garden design, the wealth and power of the owner could be conveyed, as well as providing an area for sensual delight.

 22

Between 1999 and 2000 British households spent over £5 million per week on garden tools and equipment. A further £4 million was spent on garden furniture. 60

The Royal Horticultural Society in Britain has

28,000 members.

 64

Learn how to identify
pests and diseases:

 84

Leon Battista Alberti: 'We shall erect porticoes there to provide shade, arbours over which the vine can climb; we shall place vases and even amusing statues on top of marble columns, provided they are not obscene.' During the Renaissance this was the Utopian vision to which garden designers aspired. Nature was required to take a prescribed form, abiding by the laws of both art and science.

25

'Oldfield, Merry Hall, the lilies – they were inseparable. The old man, the old house, the white flowers. I should never be able to think of the one without the other, for he had been standing by the regales on the first magic day – seven years ago, it was – when I crept through the deserted garden, a trespasser, little realising that this was to be my home for many happy years.' Beverly Nichols

 108

Sources : Promojardin, SOFRES, INSEE

'Season of mists and mellow fruitfulness!
Close bosom-friend of the maturing sun;
Conspiring with him how to load and bless
With fruit the vines that round the
thatch-eaves run;
To bend with apples the moss'd
cottage trees,
And fill all fruit with ripeness to the core.'

John Keats 110

To replace a damaged part of your lawn,

cut out the
damaged patch,
turn it over and
reseed.

 76

'Detail is abandoned, and replaced by the most extreme simplicity, creating a completely natural scene. These are things that cannot be conveyed with hundreds of brush strokes. Here one or two strokes are enough. This is what is known as true subtlety.'

 33

Watching your own vegetables grow and then harvesting them gives the deepest satisfaction to any gardener. ▷ 92

The tomato contains **90%** water and **3–4%** sugar. ▷ 94

Garlic, which originates in Asia, is composed of 10–20 axillary buds, or cloves.

The first

flowers are heralds of spring;

flowering bulbs should be planted in the autumn.

 68

Planting rosebushes,
pruning and
grafting fruit trees,
taking cuttings or
layering young
plants...
Small jobs that
any novice
gardener can do.

 70

A green environment
a balcony can become an outlet
for passionate gardeners living in
the city. Containers, terracotta
pots, hanging baskets, trellises or
even a pergola can be installed –
take your pick.

 90

Acid or alkaline? pH values,
climate, aspect, altitude ...
Have you analysed the
nature of the site
before planning
your garden?

 100

Sowing:
scattered from the palm
of your hand, seeds can
turn into a colourful
bouquet or a harvest
of vegetables. This is
true creativity.

 66

In January
order your seeds and plan
your vegetable garden
for a July harvest!

 94

Your neighbour mows his lawn early every Sunday morning; your terrace is regularly flooded by someone watering pots on the floor above; your magnificent view over the lake is obscured by a tall hedge – what are your legal rights?

 104

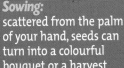

The construction of the Chinese garden did not conform to any mathematical equation. The style evolved from a system of representation that relied on the juxtaposition of views with winding paths and endless small variations on the same general theme.

*The **Islamic garden**, with its lush vegetation and abundant use of water, created a stark contrast to the sun-baked, arid environment beyond its enclosing walls. This style of garden design spread far beyond the landscape of deserts and oases, without ever losing its **intrinsic characteristics**.*

 30

The industrial revolution transformed Britain's predominantly agricultural population to a largely urban one. Rapid, unplanned industrialisation and a rising population resulted in chaos in Britain's cities, where the majority of the population lived in relentless squalor, without fresh air to breathe, space to exercise or even a view of the open sky.

 36

The vegetable garden is a feast in every sense of the word – there is nothing quite like the taste of fresh, home-grown vegetables.

 92

*The havoc wreaked by the machine on the untamed countryside of nineteenth-century Europe resulted in a profound separation between man and nature. With the advent of the **industrial revolution**, man left nature behind for good, turning to it only as an occasional spectacle on his travels.*
This development put an end to man's relationship with the soil, which, until then, had been integral to his daily life.

 36

During the Baroque period the spirit of the Renaissance lived on. Designers continued to rely on inspiration from the ancient world, to use geometric forms and to seek a dialogue with nature. The garden landscape represented an astonishing synthesis between scientific discovery, financial power and political will.

▶ 25

Chicken with watercress

Crisp and peppery, watercress awaits rediscovery in the kitchen. Cook a chicken fillet in the normal way, cover it thickly with watercress and pop it into a medium oven for 4 minutes. The result is delicious. The cress leaves will be warm whilst remaining crunchy. Recipes of a bygone era...

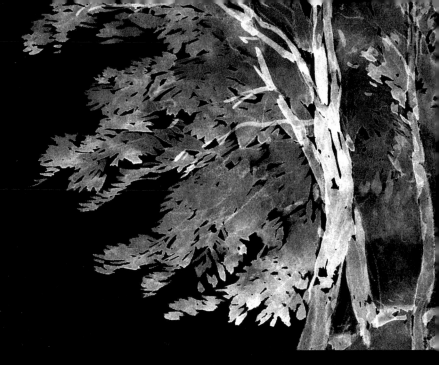

DISCOVER

OVER THE CENTURIES, MAN HAS MANIPULATED THE NATURAL LANDSCAPE TO
CREATE GARDENS REFLECTING CONTEMPORARY PHILOSOPHY, ART AND RELIGIOUS
BELIEF. THE ANCIENT GREEKS SAW THE GARDEN OF PHILOSOPHY AS THE IDEAL,
WHILE THE CHINESE TREATED THE GARDEN AS A MINIATURE, ABSTRACT VERSION
OF THE NATURAL WORLD. ARCHITECTURE AND GEOMETRY WERE KEY ELEMENTS
IN THE ITALIAN RENAISSANCE GARDEN, AND IN 17TH-CENTURY FRANCE, LE NÔTRE
TOOK THE SUN AS HIS EMBLEM AT VERSAILLES.

PARADISI IN SOLE
Paradisus Terrestris.
Or
A Garden of all sorts of pleasant flowers which our

The biblical story of Genesis, one of the fundamental stories in human culture, opens with the tale of Adam and Eve in the Garden of Eden. As Eve is tempted and plucks the apple, the forbidden fruit, from the tree of knowledge mankind is plunged on its inexorable downward spiral of sin.

Food is man's first need, and from the time of the earliest historical records the life of the human race has centred around the production of food. Our first ancestors were not farmers in the sense that we understand today. They did not sow seeds or cultivate the land. They lived an uncertain, hand-to-mouth existence, hunting wild animals, gathering nuts and berries and digging up edible roots. At some point, however, someone must have decided to catch and tame some of the wild animals that they hunted, and someone else thought of sowing seeds from the plants that they ate. This was the beginning of agriculture as we know it today – although the methods were still very primitive indeed.

THE NEOLITHIC AGRICULTURAL REVOLUTION

The advent of the forest garden 10,000 years ago heralded an agricultural revolution in Neolithic times. The cultivation of cereal crops was revolutionary and marked a decisive stage in people's relationship with their environment. The first farmers abandoned their nomadic lifestyle so that they could tend their crops. They rejected the hazards associated with the life of a hunter-gatherer, and this change reflected a new level of intellectual development. In order to sow seed, some degree of understanding of the process of germination and growth was essential. These early farmers also had to recognise the changes of the seasons, as seed could only be sown successfully at the appropriate time of year. The original sinner in the Garden of Eden thus became a gardener. Through the propagation of crops, humans embraced both sky and earth, making themselves masters of the elements. The word for paradise in Persian is *perdaz*, meaning 'enclosure'. The garden paradise was separated from the untamed world. The abundance that resulted from a combination of hard labour and knowledge needed to be protected. Cultivated by human hands, the garden became an idealised version of the natural world, and humankind's relationship with it came to be seen as a reflection of its relationship with the world at large. In every civilisation the garden forms a dialogue between man and the universe.

ADAM AND EVE

Earthly paradise is a garden. Bibliothèque National, Paris.

THE LEGEND OF CREATION

The ancient Egyptian story of the division of the waters and the Earth is closely related to that of the Book of Genesis in the Bible. Nun, the expanse of primitive waters, covered everything, until the day when Shu, the god of air and light, separated the Earth, Geb, from the sky, Nut. The creation of the plants and animals representing the fertile forces of the universe followed. In Sumer, a district of ancient Babylonia, the division of the primordial elements was also cited as the origin of the world. Enki, the creator, removed the sky from the Earth and sowed the seeds of humanity. India's philosophical texts describe a similar event. In the beginning the waters reigned supreme, and from these waters the goddess Prajapati emerged, giving birth to the Earth and the sky. In the Chinese tradition men were created from silt, while in Japan the traditional myths are linked to the wind, which changes an ear of yellow corn into a man and an ear of white corn into a woman. In the Islamic tradition, the Koran describes Allah, the great gardener 'who created the firmament and the Earth and caused the rain to fall from the sky, and with the rain made very beautiful gardens grow ...'

The Greek myths associate the cultivation of the soil with the birth of mankind. Uranus, the Sky, was the lover of Gaea, the Earth. One of their sons, Cronus, rebelled and castrated his father. An oracle told Deucalion and his wife Pyrrha, sole survivors of the flood, that the Earth would become fertile once more if they threw 'the bones of their first ancestor' over their shoulders. Deucalion solved the oracle's riddle. His ancestor was none other than Gaea, the Earth, and so the 'bones' were stones that lay on the ground. He and Phyrra walked across the plain, throwing over their shoulders stones torn from the Earth, just as one clears a field with a view to sowing. The stones that Deucalion threw were transformed into men while Phyrra's became women, and in this way the human race was renewed after the devastation of the flood. By growing crops, mankind took symbolic control of fertility and deciphered one of Nature's great secrets. Pascal, the French mathematician, in sombre reflection on 'original sin', linked the Garden of Eden to that of Golgotha: 'Jesus is in a garden, but not one of delights like the first Adam, in which he and the whole of mankind were lost, but in a garden of torture where he saved himself and the whole of mankind.' This bitter view is tempered by that of Mark Twain, who believed: 'Everywhere Eve was to be found, so was Eden.'

SEPARATION OF THE EARTH AND THE SKY
Egyptian sarcophagus, Thebes necropolis, twenty-first dynasty, 10th century BC. Egyptian Museum, Turin.

GARDENS OF MYTHOLOGY

The great empires of the world owe their prosperity to the cultivation of cereal crops. There were many gardens in the ancient capital cities of Egypt, Persia and Mesopotamia. Some were used for producing crops, some were sacred sites, and others were purely ornamental. In these regions, where rainfall was rare, humans did their utmost to improve the yield of their crops,

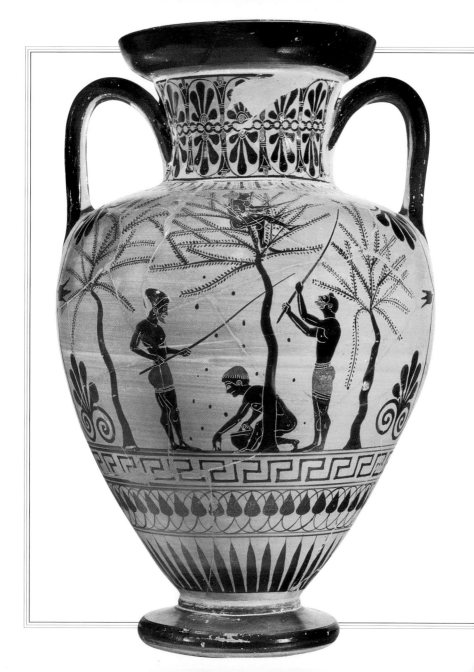

lessen the harmful effect of droughts and guarantee the success of the harvests. The need for irrigation induced them to work wonders of engineering, digging mile after mile of canals, hauling tons of soil and constructing hydraulic machines to pump water from distant rivers. The Hanging Gardens of Babylon were one of the Seven Wonders of the ancient world. Agriculture was celebrated in every art form, it was a source of inspiration for the decorative arts, poetry and was even represented in funeral rites. In Persia the great kings had vast areas set aside as parks and some of the land was dedicated to raising game that would become prey for royal hunts. In his book *Economics*, the Greek historian Xenophon praised Cyrus, the Persian gardener-monarch and commander of vast territories. Cyrus constantly worked on his own land, and one day Lysander came to him and said: 'Really Cyrus, I am filled with wonder at the sight of all this beauty, but I admire even more the person who designed and laid out this garden for you.' Cyrus, delighted by his words, replied: 'Well, it was I who designed and laid it all out; there are even some trees I have planted. Are you surprised, Lysander? I swear to you by Mithras, that when I am feeling well, I never sit down to dine without having worked up a sweat while labouring at some rustic task.' After the fall of these great civilisations, the legends of the great 'paradise gardens' that they had created lived on.

THE OLIVE HARVEST
Men appropriate the Earth. Greek amphora. British Museum, London.

THE NATURAL GARDENS OF THE GREEKS

The ancient Greeks preferred the natural landscape to cultivated gardens, but they played a vital role in garden history by compiling written records about the vast gardens built by the Persians and Egyptians. The Romans, who were inclined to build colossal structures to boost their self-esteem, read these descriptions and drew inspiration from them, as did the garden designers of Renaissance Europe. However, grand, sumptuous garden creations were rare in the Greek world, where gardens could take the form of orchards or shrines offered to the gods, open-air courtyards where the great philosophers taught their pupils, or areas set aside for sport and exercise. In the *Odyssey* Homer evokes the beauty of the garden of Ithaca, the birth-place of Odysseus. The strength of Odysseus' attachment to his native soil is expressed in the scene where he proves to his father, Laertes, that he is really his son by listing all the trees his father gave him: 'I can tell you all the trees you gave me one day in this garden terrace ... We wound our way through these very trees, you told me all their names. You gave me 13 pear trees, 10 apple trees, and 40 fig trees and at the same time, you pointed out the 50 rows of vines that were to be mine.' In spite of this deep-rooted attachment to the land, no great landscape projects were ever carried out in any of the major cities, such as Athens.

DEMETER, GODDESS OF THE HARVEST, AND PERSEPHONE, AROUND WHOM THE SEASONS TURN

Over the centuries, humankind built up a body of knowledge around efficient cultivation practices, handed down from generation to generation. It was the common belief that the gods played a part in the fertility of the soil and the changing seasons. Greek myths are rich in allegorical interpretations of the forces that preside over the mysteries of life and death. Demeter, goddess of fertility, known in Roman mythology as Ceres, was the first to cut through the Earth, using her curved ploughshare. As Mother Earth, she was the source of plant life and the goddess of the harvest. She was also the mother of Persephone, whose fate it was to be carried off by Hades, god of the Underworld. This was a catastrophic event, both for Persephone's parents and for the world at large. As soon as she descended into the Underworld a long drought began, during which nothing grew on the Earth. Demeter travelled all over the world, searching desperately for Persephone. At one point she was helped by some peasants, so to thank them she gave a handful of corn to their son, which, as a divine gift, he was obliged to sow. Eventually Zeus, Persephone's father, snatched his daughter from the amorous embrace of Hades. As soon as Persephone saw the light of day the corn that had been sown by the peasant boy germinated and the Earth was fruitful once again. Hades extracted a promise from Zeus that Persephone would spend a part of each year in the Underworld with him, and to this day,

ROMAN MOSAIC

Villa Livia, fresco in garden room. Museo Nazionale Romano delle Terme, Rome.

Persephone's absence from the Earth is marked by the winter, when the frozen ground lies barren. In this way Demeter revealed the secret of the harvest to mankind, and by virtue of her return in spring Persephone guarantees a season of fertility each year.

There are other myths inspired by the theme of cultivation. Hercules, for example, was charged by King Eurystheus to bring back the golden apples from the beautiful garden of the Hesperides. To reach the garden Hercules had to travel to the western extremity of the world, overcoming many difficulties on the way. The entrance to the garden was guarded by a dragon called Ladon, which Hercules had to kill before he could pick the apples and return with them to King Eurystheus. Another story about apples described a beauty contest organised by Zeus in which Aphrodite, Hera and Athena participated. A cautious Zeus entrusted Paris, a young shepherd, with the task of choosing the most beautiful contestant. Aphrodite seduced Paris, promising him the hand of Helen if he declared her the winner. Even though Helen was already married to Menalaus, the king of Troy. Paris accepted and offered Aphrodite an apple as proof of his choice. Helen's subsequent abduction by Paris was to unleash the Trojan Wars. For all that, however, the ancient Greeks were not destined to create their own garden style. They were architects, philosophers and scientists, but they were not gardeners.

THE ROMANS, GARDENERS ON A GRAND SCALE

To the Greeks, the garden had been a place of learning. Swimming pools, shrines, gymnasiums and shaded walks combined to form a perfect environment for schools such as the Lyceum and the Academy. The Greek garden was a place in which to exercise both the mind and the body. Consequently, its design was based on human dimensions. The gardens of Rome expressed something quite different. At the height of their power, the Romans adopted the practice of previous civilisations, creating large, sophisticated gardens. They were dazzled by the descriptions of Persian and Egyptian 'paradises' that they found in books by the ancient Greek historians Xenophon and Pausanius and felt themselves fully equal to the challenge of rivalling these magnificent gardens. Although reflecting an appreciation of the poetry of nature and a communion with the fruitful Earth, they also represented opulence and pride in their gardens, using technical expertise unequalled anywhere in the world. These gardens were an expression of the power and prestige of the emperor. The decline of the Roman Empire resulted in the disappearance of the garden for a time as a place of luxury and pleasure.

THE HEAVENLY GARDEN

Mary in a garden, typical of the art of the Middle Ages, fifteenth century. Städelsches Kunstinstitut, Frankfurt.

THE CHURCH OPPOSES THE IMAGE OF THE GARDEN AS A PLACE OF PLEASURE

For ten centuries the cultivation of the soil was reduced almost entirely to a struggle against hunger. There were exceptions, of course, but with the fall of the Roman Empire extravagant garden projects came to an abrupt end. The church had a hand in this process. Wishing to do away with paganism, it made it clear that it was God who should be worshipped and not the Earth. From that moment the study of nature was reduced to practical knowledge and the principles of productive working methods. The inherent beauty of the plant world was acknowledged only in illuminated manuscripts, stained glass and the stonework of Gothic cathedrals. The walled, monastic garden, a typical feature of the medieval world, was there to provide medicinal herbs and food, but it was no longer a source of intellectual or artistic energy. Botanical science did survive, but only on a superficial level.

THE REBIRTH OF THE GARDEN

The end of the Middle Ages marked a relaxation in austerity. The castles and grand houses of the nobility were surrounded by extravagant gardens. Both the countryside and the garden

became themes for literature. The garden was a setting for romance. It was known as the 'garden of love' or the 'garden of delights'. During the 15th century the Italian Renaissance blossomed, intensifying the importance of the garden. Liberated from the terrors of the Middle Ages, intellectual curiosity was reborn, the Renaissance mind embracing everything from the movement of the stars to human anatomy. Nature was no longer a metaphor, but a living reality. Poised somewhere between architecture and landscape, the garden developed into a complete art form in its own right. Leon Battista Alberti, a great figure of the *Quattrocento* (the 15th century) set out the principles of garden design. His work, *De re aedificatoria*, defines the criteria for constructing a garden using geometry and mathematics. Under his influence, the gardener was transformed into an architect and a mathematician. This new passion for the aesthetic appeal of gardens sprang directly from Humanism, one of the most important intellectual movements of the Renaissance. No longer content to use the Christian tradition as their sole frame of reference, Humanist scholars looked to the ideals of the ancient world, where they saw the art of creating gardens glorified alongside that of building as supreme examples of genius. Nothing more was necessary. The revival of interest in the garden was part of a more general return to antiquity, to pagan forces, pleasure and leisure pursuits. Alberti described gardens as places 'whose forms resemble those we give our houses, circles, semicircles or figures of the same kind surrounded by laurels, cypresses and junipers with some trees planted in a straight line and pruned to form regular lines ... We shall also place rare plants there. The Ancients used boxwood parterres to write their names along the borders where they also placed aromatic plants.' Renaissance designers devoted themselves to the art of taming nature, an aim that to some extent exists to this day, as is demonstrated by the ordered planting schemes of many modern gardens. It was not until later in the history of the garden, during the Picturesque period of the 18th century, that people aspired to create landscapes that revolved around nature rather than imposing humankind's strict, aesthetic principles upon nature.

VILLA DI CASTELLO

Gardens of the Villa Medici, oil on canvas, G. Utens. Museum of Ancient Art, Florence.

ROYAL GARDENS: THE WILL OF THE KING

During the Baroque period the spirit of the Renaissance lived on. Designers continued to rely on inspiration from the ancient world, to use geometric forms and to seek a dialogue with nature. The garden landscape represented an astonishing synthesis between scientific discovery, financial power and political will.

A garden lends itself to the expression of political power. In England the Stuart monarchs of the 17th century used the garden as an explicit metaphor for the ideal world that they wanted to create for their citizens. The beautiful, cultivated landscape summoned from chaos and disorder was a symbol of the monarchy's beneficent power. The garden was also used as a political metaphor in lavish court entertainments commissioned by the Stuart Kings James I and Charles I. Inigo Jones's court masques are a particularly good example of this tradition. His stage directions are very explicit: 'The Britanides and their Prophetic Powers were to be re-established in this garden by the unanimous and magnificent virtues of the King and Queen Majesties making this land a pattern to all Nations as Greece was amongst the ancients.' As a metaphor, the garden brought the added advantage of associations with Eden. The implication was that the Stuart monarchy would create a new paradise.

When he was still a young man, French King Louis XIV commissioned André Le Nôtre to build the gardens around his palace at Versailles. Le Nôtre, whose influence was to dominate European garden design for more than a century, created a new style to demonstrate the absolute power and grandeur of the king. 17th-century designers still looked to the Renaissance for their inspiration. The gardens from which they

THE KITCHEN GARDEN
The king's kitchen garden at Versailles, according to plans drawn by La Quintinie in 1690. Bibliothèque Mazarine, Paris.

took their cue were characterised by an elaborate use of water, an open perspective and carefully calculated proportions. The difference between these gardens and those of Le Nôtre and his contemporaries was principally one of scale. The garden was not confined to the area immediately outside the house, villa or château, as there was no longer any formal constraint on its size. To some extent, this change was due to the development of science. Greater use of perspective combined with new discoveries in astronomy seemingly opened the garden up to infinity. Versailles was built to imitate the known universe, with the sun at the centre. Louis XIV, the Sun King, was the sun's living image on Earth, and the sun myth that surrounded the person of the king is the key to a full appreciation of the magnificence of Versailles. The work of Le Nôtre at Versailles was destined to be the inspiration for numerous Baroque gardens for more than a century, first in France, then in Charles II's England and Peter the Great's Russia and finally throughout Europe. The gigantic proportions of the garden alone proclaim the unprecedented extent of the king's power. The site covered 15,000 hectares (37000 acres) of reclaimed land and drained marshes, and the work involved thousands of men.

FOOLING THE EYE IN THE BAROQUE GARDEN

The use of symmetry in Baroque gardens was no longer as rigid as it had been during the Renaissance. Designers made greater use of perspective to fool the eye and to diminish the sense of distance within the landscape. This was achieved by gradually widening canals and avenues as they moved further away from the viewpoint. This form of 'slowed-down

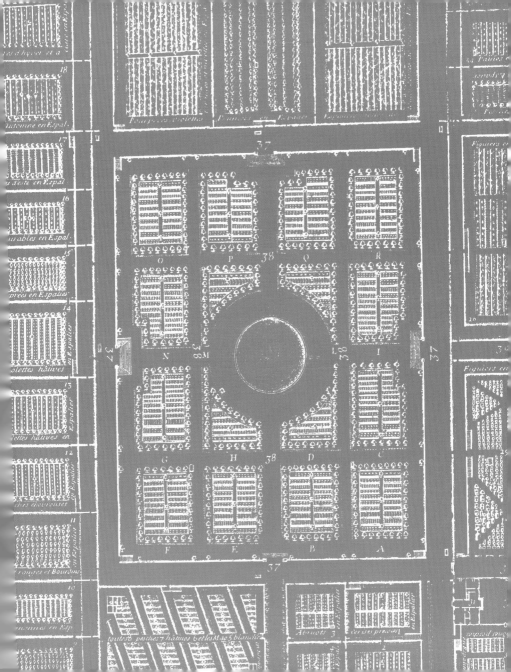

perspective' was combined with classical perspective, and together they worked to accelerate the passage of the eye through the landscape, giving visitors the impression that they were leaping forward into a visual infinity. These optical games shook up ordinary perceptions and gave the garden visitor a sense of contemplating the 'infinite spaces' described by Pascal, the brilliant 17th-century French mathematician. The same optical illusions characterised all the great gardens of the period. Le Nôtre's version of the French garden was imitated all over Europe. King Charles II of England, Louis XIV's first cousin, asked if he might borrow Le Nôtre. He wanted him to come to England and transform the park at Greenwich into a landscape that would equal the gardens of Versailles, as well as redesigning St James's Park in London. In the event, Le Nôtre made a series of drawings for the improvement of Greenwich Park, which have been preserved, but there is no record that he ever came to England himself. In the end it was André Mollet, son of the head gardener at the Tuileries in Paris, and his brother, Gabriel, who were employed to design the grounds of both St James's Park and Hampton Court. They imposed formal avenues, walks, lines of trees and canals over the existing meadows. Charles II, like Louis XIV, believed in the absolute power of the monarchy, and the avenue was a fitting metaphor for him to use. It suggested a power centred on the palace and radiating outwards into the world beyond. The canal in St James's Park was made by joining together several existing ponds. One of the ponds, originally known as the Cowford Pond, was dug out to make a formal pool, which was renamed Rosamond's Pool. It became a famous haunt for lovers, but also unfortunately attracted many suicides before being filled in during 1770.

EDMUND WALLER AND THE GARDEN AT HALL BARN

THE GARDENS OF THE ALHAMBRA

At Grenada (13th and 14th centuries), Timothy Easton.

After travelling in France and Italy with John Evelyn, the poet Edmund Waller returned to England in 1651. He embarked at once on planning a garden in the French style for Hall Barn, his estate in Buckinghamshire. To this day, Hall Barn has a formal canal garden covering approximately 7.5 acres (3 hectares) immediately outside the house. A further 20 acres (8 hectares) were planted with woodland, which was cut through with groves and avenues in the French style. These radiated from a domed rotunda called the Temple of Venus and were used as shady, sheltered walks, as walking had become a fashionable pastime for the nobility, made popular by Charles II, and was now as common an activity in parks as riding, carriage driving or hunting. Waller worked on the garden for more than 35 years. The layout was completed after his death by his grandson, Harry Waller, and his stepfather, John Aislabie, who went on to create the garden at Studley Royal in North Yorkshire. An avenue planted in 1730 to lead to an obelisk was the last feature to be installed.

THE GARDENS OF ALLAH

The Islamic garden, with its lush vegetation and abundant use of water, created a stark contrast to the sun-baked, arid environment beyond its enclosing walls. This style of garden design spread far beyond the landscape of deserts and oases, without ever losing its intrinsic characteristics. Wherever it appeared, the Muslim garden gave the impression of great ingenuity, while also conveying a sense of permanence. It was a shrine to the memory of Byzantine splendour and to the Mogul courts in which the style was originally forged. Between the 13th and the 17th centuries, the Islamic style of garden design spread across the world, from the Atlantic to the Bay of Bengal. Fabulous sites, such as the Alhambra to the west and the Taj Mahal to the east, bear witness to an astonishing blend of cultures, a successful synthesis that benefited from the contributions of three continents – Europe, Africa and India. The Arabian world stood at the crossroads of three continents, and the Muslim message was carried across the world by merchants and soldiers. From 650 AD, their armies gained a foothold in Mesopotamia, Palestine, Syria and Egypt. In 750 the territories of central Asia, the Mediterranean coast, North Africa and, finally, the Iberian peninsula were conquered. It is a mark of the strength of the invaders that, though all these countries were taken by force and could naturally be expected to resist the imposition of foreign culture, the Muslims made a lasting impression on them – particularly with their use of water, which lay at the heart of Muslim culture and engineering. The Arabs invariably improved the water resources of the countries that they invaded, which made a huge and unforgettable contribution to the local way of life. The remains of the hydraulic systems can still be seen in the archaeological remains of the first great Islamic gardens. Traces of canal networks stretching over several kilometres have been uncovered, and constructions such as tanks, artificial lakes, diversion dams and artesian wells formed part of a vast irrigation system used for watering orchards, crops and pleasure gardens.

GARDEN OF FIDELITY
Mogul manuscript.
Victoria and Albert
Museum, London.

TRUE DIALOGUE BETWEEN THE REAL
AND THE METAPHYSICAL WORLDS

In the Muslim religion it was taboo to create images of man or beast. As a result, Islamic artists were forced to invent an abstract language of forms and signs. Only in this way they were able to represent mankind and reveal his position in the cosmos.

The Islamic garden was humankind's attempt to reconstruct the natural world through the use of science. Mathematics, in the form of algebra, arithmetic, trigonometry and geometry, were

درختهای انار هم هست کرد او حوض تمام سه برکه را

at the core of the design process, as was astronomy. The pure forms of the garden were given validity by the disciplines of science, and the garden served as a fulcrum for an exchange between the real and the metaphysical worlds. In the same way, botany defined the flower as a collection of geometric forms, from the simple to the complex. To decipher its appearance was to discover a living code. Science approached the world from the same angle: the desire to discover the structure behind mathematics, biology and astronomy.

In Spain the Muslim tradition was to endure for six centuries. Seville, Cordoba, Grenada, Toledo, Saragossa and Valencia still reflect the splendour of the Muslim presence, the achievement of their architects and engineers and the discoveries of their scientists. Their influence elsewhere in Europe was to endure throughout the Middle Ages.

THE IMPERIAL CHINESE GARDENS

Francis Bacon described the gardens of Imperial China as 'the highest form of art in any civilisation'. The Chinese emperors were dedicated to the art of garden design as the garden was seen as a fitting vehicle for the expression of wealth and power. As a result of this close bond between political power and garden design, the Imperial garden acts as a mirror to the long and turbulent history of the country. In the seventh century Emperor Yang Di began the construction of the Western Park garden, where the chief attraction consisted of animated figures marching along the canals and relating episodes of Chinese history. This display relied on some very sophisticated engineering, anticipating by nearly a millennium the water-powered automata that became so fashionable in the gardens of Renaissance Europe. In the centuries that followed, Xüan Zung constructed the Garden of the Magnificent Clear Lake in honour of a concubine, and Huizong devoted years to the garden of the Lake of the Clarity of Gold. The tradition of garden making was revived after the Mongolian invasions, when Chinese power was restored under the Ming emperors. Under the Qing Dynasty (1644–1911) the Imperial garden enjoyed a new Golden Age. The emperor Qianlong (1736–1799), turning his passion for gardens into a way of life, earned himself the nickname of 'the gardener emperor'. The famous gardens of Chengde, which were his enduring legacy, cover at least 560 hectares (1,385 acres). The magnificence of these Imperial gardens gave them a status in their own right, which went far beyond the simple expression of political power.

GARDENS NO BIGGER THAN A MUSTARD SEED

The gardens of China's educated classes were encoded with complex religious and philosophical messages. They were a space in which to meditate, a living landscape painting. To poets and art enthusiasts, the garden was the reflection of an intellectual universe whose subtlety revealed just enough to cause visitors to be overwhelmed by their own insignificance. It gave concrete form to the abstract emotions, ephemeral sensations and profound ideas that painting and poetry also endeavoured to capture. The *Manual for painting gardens no bigger than a mustard seed* conveys an idea of the sophistication of Chinese gardens: 'People without eyes should feel as if they could see; people without ears should feel as if they could hear. Detail is abandoned, and replaced by the most extreme simplicity, creating a completely natural scene. These are things that cannot be conveyed with hundreds of brush strokes. Here one or two strokes are enough. This is what is known as true subtlety.'

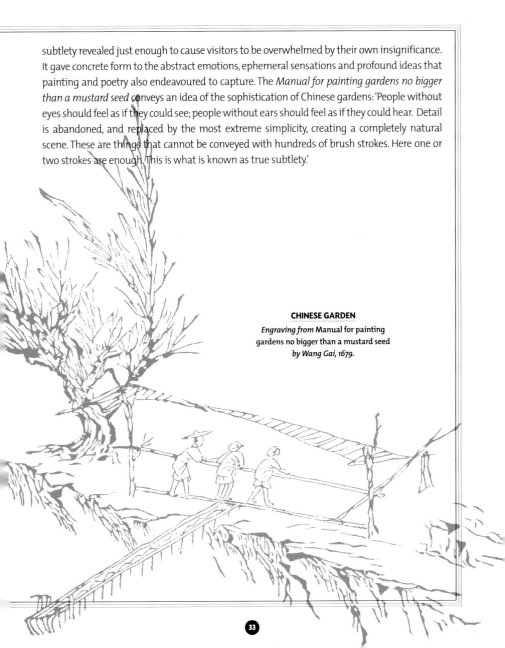

CHINESE GARDEN

Engraving from Manual for painting gardens no bigger than a mustard seed *by Wang Gai, 1679.*

The aim of the Chinese garden design can be encapsulated in just one short phrase: to paint the invisible with a couple of elusive strokes. Three dominant cultures – Taoism, Confucianism and Buddhism – were at the heart of this simple approach. It was not enough to present the eye with a vision of nature, it also had to be possible to discern evidence of the mysteries in the forces of nature. The garden must possess two elements of perfect simplicity: the surface of water and the raised stone. Water is the fluid element, warm and feminine; the rock is the hard element, dry, masculine and still. The pride inherent in rock is slowly eroded by energetic water, the passive nature of minerals yielding to the sheer force of the movement and the vital rhythm of the water. These were truths that the Chinese liked to contemplate: 'The stones are the bones of the mountains and the waterfalls are the bones of the stones. It is said that the nature of water is weak – how could it be called a bone? I reply: it strikes the mountains and penetrates the stones; its power shakes the high mountains; there is nothing stronger than water.'

The conflict between mountain and water was a central theme in China, endlessly explored in poetry and painting. Wang Gai said: 'By gazing at the autumn clouds, my mind takes flight and floats. In meeting with the spring breeze, my thoughts flow like a great and powerful current. Even the music of instruments and the riches of jade cannot equal this pleasure.'

THE SPIRIT OF NATURE REVEALED IN THE CHINESE GARDEN

The question of a linear perspective, based on optics and geometry, occupied the European garden designer's mind for many years. In China, however, it never arose. The concepts peculiar to Buddhism and Taoism led to the creation of gardens that claimed their own space, independent of any abstract definitions of scale or perspective. The construction of the Chinese garden did not conform to any mathematical equation. The style evolved from a system of representation that relied on the juxtaposition of views with winding paths and endless small variations on the same general themes. Subtle hints or suggestions were at the core of the Chinese garden, as the overall aim was to reveal the spirit of nature rather than nature itself. To walk through one of these gardens was to dissociate oneself from reality, free oneself from imposed structure and abandon the superficial. Proportions themselves were not considered important. A large rock could be placed next to a dwarf tree to represent a mountain. Scale, to the Chinese mind, was only an approximation of truth, sensation was all.

The use of bonsai trees in gardens built on a miniature scale was a Japanese development of the Chinese style. Confronted by excess, Buddha said: 'The whole universe is hidden in a single seed.' To grasp the profound meaning of this statement is to appreciate Chinese gardens in all their grandeur and subtlety.

20TH-CENTURY GARDENS – THE INDUSTRIAL AGE

The havoc wreaked by machine on the untamed countryside of 19th-century Europe resulted in a profound split between man and nature. This development put an end to man's relationship with the soil, which, until then, had been integral to his daily life. The expansion of industry also had an unprecedented impact on the natural landscape. The countryside was enveloped by creeping urbanisation as smoking factory chimneys, gas lights, roads and railway lines changed the face of vast areas of the landscape for ever. Thousands of people abandoned the countryside and went to work in mines or factories. At every level of society there developed a nostalgia for horizons composed of fields, woods and rivers. People had put nature behind them. Eventually, the populations of large urban areas sought to rediscover their former quality of life and to reclaim their rights to fresh air, clean water and sunlight. New spaces were created by town planners – the great town parks, individual gardens in the poorer suburbs, and allotments.

AN ENGLISH PARK
Detail of Regent's Park, William Callow (1812–1908). Victoria and Albert Museum, London.

GREEN SPACES – THE LUNGS OF THE CITY

After the industrial revolution the majority of the urban population lived in relentless squalor, without fresh air, space to exercise or even a view of the open sky. The death rate in the city was considerably higher than that in the country. By 1833 the House of Commons was beginning to discuss the need to improve the conditions of the working classes. An urgent need for open spaces for exercise and walks was identified. John Claudius Loudon, the Scottish author and landscape designer, went on a tour of Europe and noticed that most foreign cities had public parks, either created and maintained by their government or thrown open to the public by the Crown. He admired the boulevards and parks of Paris, which he referred to as 'breathing zones'. He was also impressed by the promenades, public gardens and royal parks of Germany, all of which were open to the general public. In London, by comparison, there was not a single space preserved as a park or a public walk from Limehouse in the east to Regent's Park in the north. On his return, Loudon dedicated himself to the cause of establishing new parks. Although much of his work went unacknowledged, he sowed the seed for the green spaces of the future. In 1833 the subject of green spaces in London was taken up in parliament and by all the newspapers. A Select Committee was formed 'for an enquiry into the means of providing open spaces in the vicinity of populous towns as public walks and places of exercise, calculated to

W. Orton

Greenwich Park

promote the health and happiness and comfort of the inhabitants'. Despite the findings of the committee, for many years parks continued to be founded and maintained by private benefactors.

ALLOTMENTS – GARDENS FOR THE WORKERS

During the reign of Elizabeth I, acts of parliament were passed that allowed common land to be enclosed. This movement began gradually, but between 1760 and 1818 over 2 million hectares (4,900,000 acres) of common land in Britain was enclosed and incorporated into the estates of large landowners. Deprived of their source of food and income, the landless poor found jobs on large estates or migrated to the big industrial cities to find work in factories. A handful of landowners understood their plight and, believing that too much had been taken from the peasants, set aside parcels of land that could be used by the poor to cultivate food. This was the beginning of the allotment movement.

In the 1860s 30,000 people were estimated to garden on 10,000 plots on an area above London known as Hunger Hill. There are still allotments on Hunger Hill today. In 1860, these gardeners organised the first ever rose show in Britain.

At the outbreak of war in 1914 there were 6 million allotments in England and Wales. Special powers granted under the Defence of the Realm Act allowed local councils to requisition land. As a result, a further 1.5 million plots were created. These were all cultivated by recruits to the 'Every-man-a-gardener' campaign. During the Second World War the 'Dig for Victory' campaign resulted in a similar return to the land. The allotments were estimated to have produced nearly 1.5 million tons of food during the course of the war.

In peace time the allotment movement has declined dramatically. Over the past decade much of the land set aside for allotments outside cities has been bought from cash-starved local authorities by developers. Nevertheless, it is estimated that 300,000 British households still grow their own food on an allotment.

A RETURN TO NATURE

In America large urban parks were created. These green spaces were seen as vehicle for the spiritual regeneration that could be achieved through communion with nature. Later on, this notion was to lead to the creation of National Parks and Reserves, first in North America and then in Europe. In this case, however, it was nature itself that needed to be saved from pollution. For the first time, a nature unsullied by any interference from humans became the ideal.

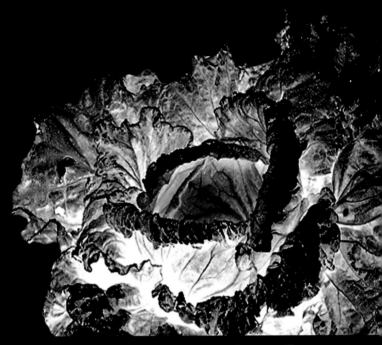

LOOK

AT WORK AND AT PLAY ON ALLOTMENTS. FROM TINY SQUARES OF LAND GROWING PEAS AND BEANS TO ROWS OF ORNAMENTAL CABBAGE, DELPHINIUMS AND RASPBERRY CANES, TOPPED AND TAILED WITH A GREENHOUSE AND POTTING SHED, THE ALLOTMENT MAKES THE JOYS OF GARDENING POSSIBLE, EVEN FOR URBAN APARTMENT-DWELLERS.

The real discipline is to pick the strawberries without eating a single one. (Doug Larson)

Successful gardening is not a question of wealth. It is a question of love, taste and knowledge (Vita Sackville-West)

Sing of the gardens, my heart, which you do not know;

The gardens fused as if in glass, clear, beyond reach... (Rainer Maria Rilke)

A garden is a lovesome thing, God wot! (Thomas Edward Brown)

Our bodies are our gardens, to which our wills are gardeners. (William Shakespeare)

He who throws weeds into his neighbour's garden, shall see them grow in his own garden. (Russian proverb)

Love is a blade of wild grass and not a garden plant. (Ippolito Nievo)

You are a full-spread, fair-set vine, And can with tendrils love entwine, Yet dried ere you distil your wine (Robert Herrick

Gardens are a kind of dream, like poems, music and algebra. (Hector Bianciotti)

After all, who is God? An eternal child playing an eternal game in an eternal garden. (Shri Aurobindo)

Where are the blooms of Summer? In the West,

Blushing their last to the last sunny hours, (Thomas Hood)

Mysterious garden of my distant childhood, an enchanted kingdom lost on the horizon. (Fernanda de Castro)

Let patience grow in your garden (John Heywood)

There grew pied wind-flowers and violets; Daisies, those pearl'd Acturi of the earth,

240

The constellated flower that never sets; (Percy Bysshe Shelley)

More things grow in a garden than the gardener sows there (Spanish proverb)

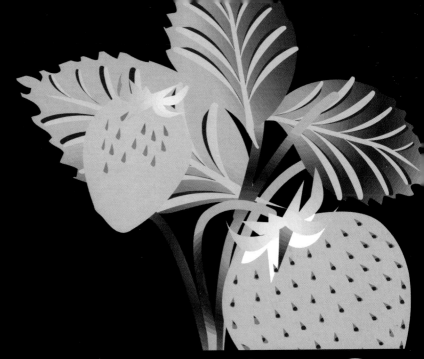

IN PRACTICE

GARDENING LEAVES NOTHING TO CHANCE. EVERY PLANT, VEGETABLE AND FRUIT MUST BE SOWN, PLANTED, CUT, PRUNED AND PICKED IN ACCORDANCE WITH WELL-DEFINED RULES. A GARDENER TAKES PRIDE IN WATCHING HIS GARDEN FLOURISH AND IN HARVESTING THE PRODUCE FROM HIS VEGETABLE PLOT; HE'LL HAVE LEARNED HOW TO TAME, BUT MOST IMPORTANTLY, TO RESPECT NATURE.

The gardener's tools

It is important to wear comfortable, roomy clothes when you are gardening. Anything tight at the waistband or shoulders will restrict your movements, making it uncomfortable to stretch or bend. An apron with large pockets to hold secateurs or packets of seeds is very useful, as is an old cushion or pad to kneel on.

Quality above all else

Gardening calls for an array of tools. Go for quality – a good tool is easier to handle and lasts longer. Tools for working the soil should have good blades and strong, wooden handles.

To the untrained eye, cutting tools can all look much the same. In fact, using the wrong tool can cause damage. Taking hedge trimmers to a rosebush, for example, may well damage its branches.

The right position

For work carried out standing upright, choose tools to suit your height. Make sure it feels comfortable before you buy it. The wrong length of handle causes back strain. Kneel rather than bend down when sowing or weeding as this is the best way to garden without aches and pains.

Maintenance

Tools should be inspected and cleaned each time they are used. Clean blades with a piece of wood (not stone or metal) rather than water, and then wipe with an oily rag. Sharpen blades regularly, but take care not to cut yourself. When not in use, tools should stand vertically in a rack, with the handle facing downwards. By observing these rules, you'll ensure that your tools will last for many years.

A good gardener's apron should be equipped with several pockets to carry tools and seed packets.

Equip yourself with at least two pairs of gloves, a lightweight pair for general work and a thicker pair for heavier jobs.

Choose secateurs with a clean cut, whose blades won't leave ragged wounds on the stems.

A watering can is perfect for getting water to the base of the plants.

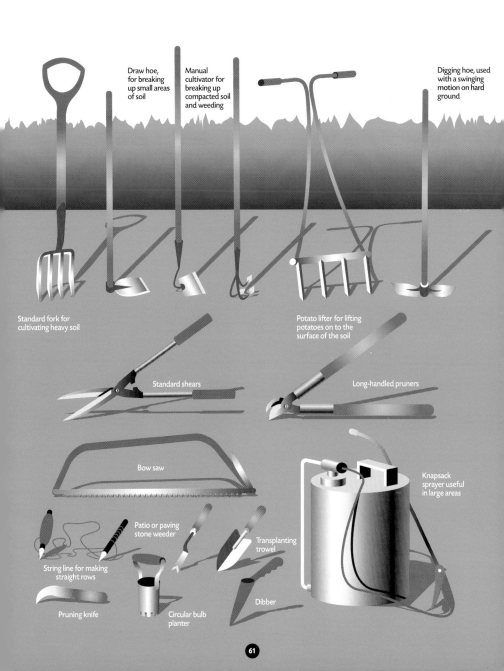

Draw hoe, for breaking up small areas of soil

Manual cultivator for breaking up compacted soil and weeding

Digging hoe, used with a swinging motion on hard ground

Standard fork for cultivating heavy soil

Potato lifter for lifting potatoes on to the surface of the soil

Standard shears

Long-handled pruners

Bow saw

Knapsack sprayer useful in large areas

Patio or paving stone weeder

Transplanting trowel

String line for making straight rows

Pruning knife

Circular bulb planter

Dibber

The plant families

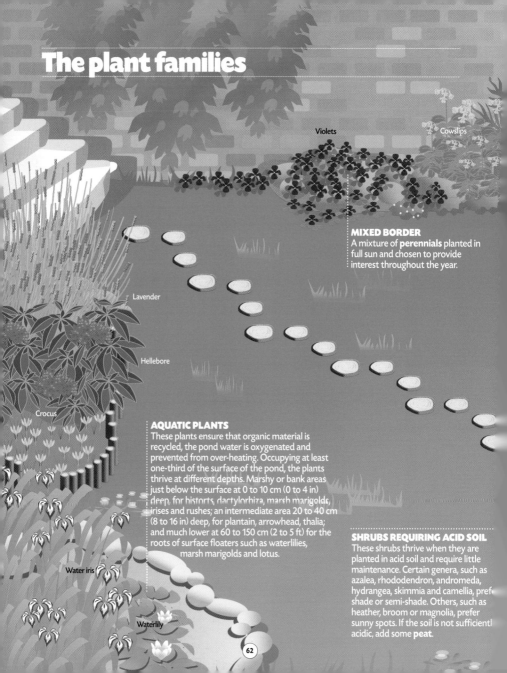

Violets

Cowslips

MIXED BORDER
A mixture of **perennials** planted in full sun and chosen to provide interest throughout the year.

Lavender

Hellebore

Crocus

AQUATIC PLANTS
These plants ensure that organic material is recycled, the pond water is oxygenated and prevented from over-heating. Occupying at least one-third of the surface of the pond, the plants thrive at different depths. Marshy or bank areas just below the surface at 0 to 10 cm (0 to 4 in) deep, for bistorts, dactylorhiza, marsh marigolds, irises and rushes; an intermediate area 20 to 40 cm (8 to 16 in) deep, for plantain, arrowhead, thalia; and much lower at 60 to 150 cm (2 to 5 ft) for the roots of surface floaters such as waterlilies, marsh marigolds and lotus.

Water iris

Waterlily

SHRUBS REQUIRING ACID SOIL
These shrubs thrive when they are planted in acid soil and require little maintenance. Certain genera, such as azalea, rhododendron, andromeda, hydrangea, skimmia and camellia, prefe shade or semi-shade. Others, such as heather, broom or magnolia, prefer sunny spots. If the soil is not sufficientl acidic, add some **peat**.

Ivy

Berberis

Ferns

Campanula

Daffodils

Dwarf
conifers

Rose

Gazania

ROCK PLANTS

By nature economical, these plants prefer clay soils, require little fertiliser and can thrive in difficult conditions. Living in the spaces between rocks, they nevertheless require good drainage. When creating a rockery, mix some fine gravel or even coarse sand into the soil, as this will allow the water to filter through. Choose plants that form a carpet, are no taller than 35 cm (14 in) and can be mixed with more established plants.

CLIMBING PLANTS

Plants with decorative foliage and flowers generally prefer cool and well-drained soils. Never buy a climbing plant with bare roots. Sun-loving: the annuals (nasturtium, morning glory, sweet pea); the perennials (everlasting pea); climbers (honeysuckle, clematis, wisteria, passion flower, roses, solanum, Virginia creeper, summer jasmine, roses, trachelospermum). Semi-shade: (hop, perennial honeysuckle, climbing hydrangea, jasmine, ivy).

Jasmine

Magnolia

Camellia

Plan your garden

The walled garden

The walled garden dates back to the tradition of medieval enclosures. The wall gives shelter to fruit and vegetables, delicate flowers and medicinal or aromatic plants. The wall usually encloses an area of around 200 to 400 square metres (240 to 480 square yards) and so is usually found in the larger garden. Install a stone bench and allow moss to cover the wall, and your walled garden will become a perfectly peaceful environment.

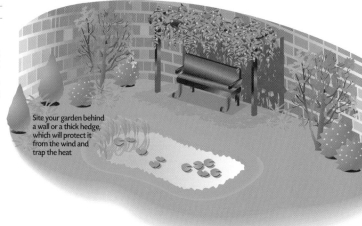

Site your garden behind a wall or a thick hedge, which will protect it from the wind and trap the heat

The wild garden

The beauty of this garden lies in the exuberant tangle of vegetation. Here, the gardener takes a back seat. The thriving hedge contains numerous species: hawthorn, hazel, dog-rose, blackberry, alder and ash. Sow clumps of cow parsley, everlasting pea, cowslip, perennial geranium, foxglove, soapwort, wallflower, and meadowsweet in a random fashion. Allow small animals to colonise a dead tree. Your garden will become a refuge for wildlife.

Attract birds by providing them with a safe haven

Install a pond, incorporating a few rocks

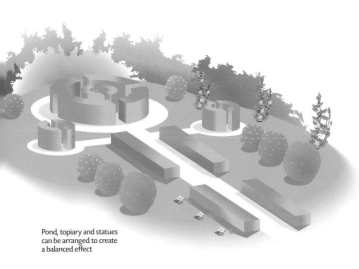

The landscaped garden

In the landscaped garden, rebellious nature is well and truly restrained. The gardens of Japan, Renaissance Italy and Tudor England left nothing to chance. Construct your design with a clear scheme in mind (an entrance, a terrace etc.). Sketch an overall plan of the site. Take the shape of trees and movement of the sun into consideration. Take the time to plan carefully, don't rush into things.

Pond, topiary and statues can be arranged to create a balanced effect

The leisure garden

Intended for relaxation, the leisure garden takes the form of a pleasant grassy area planted with fruit trees. It has large open spaces interspersed with flowering shrubs, and perennials. Climbers such as clematis, jasmine and wisteria will create a refreshing little haven.

Borders emphasize the outline of the lawn

Sowing seed

Seed is the natural way to reproduce plants and flowers. Of all gardening jobs, sowing seed can be the most rewarding. Whatever your plants, be they annuals, biennials or perennials, sow their seeds in the spring. Planting in cold frames, cloches or tunnels, however, can be carried out from February onwards.

Seeds in trays

This type of sowing is for plants that will require pricking out later (tomatoes, lettuces, cabbages, leeks, begonias).

Seeds in pots

Pots are used for growing larger seeds, two seeds being planted in each pot. If both germinate, sacrifice the weaker by cutting off the seedling at soil level.

Planting individual seeds

Plants with larger seeds, such as beans, peas and marrows, can be planted individually in small holes.

Seed drills

This method is used in the vegetable garden. Before you sow, water the drill well and use a planting tube to sow long drills.

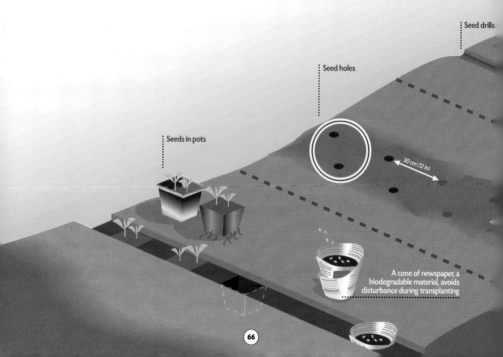

Seed drills

Seed holes

Seeds in pots

30 cm (12 in)

A cone of newspaper, a biodegradable material, avoids disturbance during transplanting

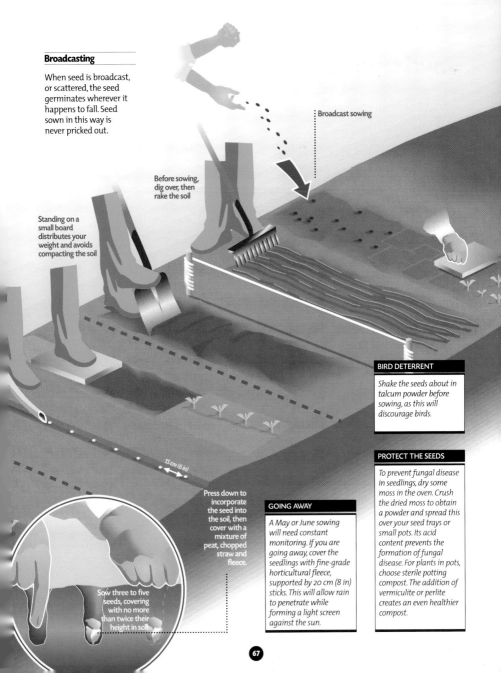

Broadcasting

When seed is broadcast, or scattered, the seed germinates wherever it happens to fall. Seed sown in this way is never pricked out.

Broadcast sowing

Before sowing, dig over, then rake the soil

Standing on a small board distributes your weight and avoids compacting the soil

15 cm (6 in)

Press down to incorporate the seed into the soil, then cover with a mixture of peat, chopped straw and fleece.

Sow three to five seeds, covering with no more than twice their height in soil.

BIRD DETERRENT

Shake the seeds about in talcum powder before sowing, as this will discourage birds.

GOING AWAY

A May or June sowing will need constant monitoring. If you are going away, cover the seedlings with fine-grade horticultural fleece, supported by 20 cm (8 in) sticks. This will allow rain to penetrate while forming a light screen against the sun.

PROTECT THE SEEDS

To prevent fungal disease in seedlings, dry some moss in the oven. Crush the dried moss to obtain a powder and spread this over your seed trays or small pots. Its acid content prevents the formation of fungal disease. For plants in pots, choose sterile potting compost. The addition of vermiculite or perlite creates an even healthier compost.

From flowering to regeneration: the lifecycle of flowering bulbs

Whether planted in a garden tub, a flower-bed or in the grass, bulbs herald the spring and can be used to brighten up the summer border. By choosing different sizes, colours and flowering times, you can create attractive corners in the garden for much of the year.

A bulb is an underground reserve of nutrients for a plant. Capable of regenerating itself during dormant periods, it can be removed from the soil and stored, once the growth above ground starts to die off. To store tender bulbs with a view to planting the following year, be sure to dig them up at the first sign of night frost. The bulbs should be lifted, cleaned and laid out on a wire rack to dry. They can then be stored in labelled paper (not plastic) bags.

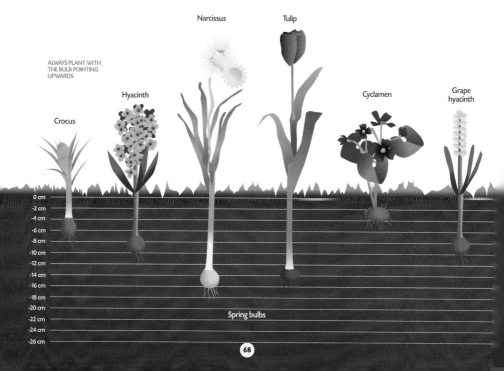

Narcissus

Tulip

ALWAYS PLANT WITH THE BULB POINTING UPWARDS

Hyacinth

Cyclamen

Grape hyacinth

Crocus

0 cm
-2 cm
-4 cm
-6 cm
-8 cm
-10 cm
-12 cm
-14 cm
-16 cm
-18 cm
-20 cm
-22 cm
-24 cm
-26 cm

Spring bulbs

Spring bulbs – regeneration

The period during which spring bulbs are for sale – from September to mid-December – corresponds to the period in which they should be planted. Flowering times range from January to May. The size of bulbs varies according to their species; nevertheless, their proportions give some idea of the eventual size that the plant will achieve. Be careful not to buy bulbs with any signs of disease, mildew or deformity. If you are not going to plant them immediately, store them in a well-ventilated place, sheltered from frost. Bulbs are not demanding: they like any soil, especially if it is well drained. If you have a really heavy clay soil you could improve it by adding peat or compost to the surface. There's nothing complicated about planting bulbs, but use a special planter which makes rounded rather than pointed holes. A pointed planter makes a tapered hole and a round bulb dropped into a hole of this shape cannot touch the bottom.

Summer bulbs – a dazzling spectacle

Summer bulbs planted in a dense carpet or mixed with perennial or annual plants, create wonderful combinations. Plant them in sunny spots. Lilies, gladioli, dahlias, oxalis, canna, agapanthus, star of Bethlehem and ranunculus will enable you to experiment with a variety of colours and flowering times ranging from May to October.

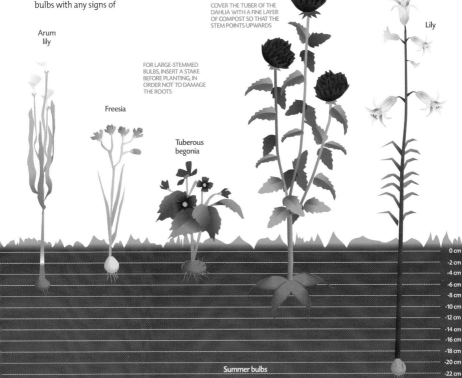

Dahlia

COVER THE TUBER OF THE DAHLIA WITH A FINE LAYER OF COMPOST SO THAT THE STEM POINTS UPWARDS

FOR LARGE-STEMMED BULBS, INSERT A STAKE BEFORE PLANTING, IN ORDER NOT TO DAMAGE THE ROOTS

Arum lily

Freesia

Tuberous begonia

Lily

Summer bulbs

0 cm
-2 cm
-4 cm
-6 cm
-8 cm
-10 cm
-12 cm
-14 cm
-16 cm
-18 cm
-20 cm
-22 cm
-24 cm
-26 cm

Planting and pruning your roses

Roses should be planted from October to March, avoiding very wet or very cold weather. Roses are available bare-rooted, free of soil or in rootball form, when the roots are still encased in the growing medium. The size of your roses will depend on their species and variety.

Winter protection

Earth up your roses, scooping out a mound of earth to cover the bud union, where the scion unites with the rootstock, usually about 5 cm (2 in) from the base of the branches. This will prevent frost damage during the winter. In the spring you should uncover the base again.

How much should you prune?

Light pruning on a weak plant encourages vigorous growth. Hard pruning on a strong plant slows vigorous growth.

When should you prune?

In the year of planting, prune as late as possible in spring. This will delay bud formation, thus avoiding frost damage. Thereafter, prune at the end of winter.

Root pruning

Carried out on roses bought with bare roots, this pruning, or trimming of the roots, ensures that the plant will thrive when it's planted.

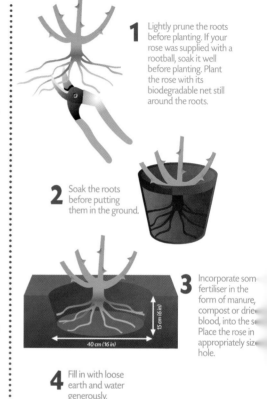

1 Lightly prune the roots before planting. If your rose was supplied with a rootball, soak it well before planting. Plant the rose with its biodegradable net still around the roots.

2 Soak the roots before putting them in the ground.

3 Incorporate som fertiliser in the form of manure, compost or drie blood, into the s Place the rose in appropriately siz hole.

15 cm (6 in)

40 cm (16 in)

4 Fill in with loose earth and water generously.

At the end of September, even up the branches of a standard rose by carrying out a light pruning

Prune above a bud, preferably on the outside of the plant

Cut

Bud

Each year in February, shorten the stems of your shrub roses

Prune large- and cluster-flowered bush roses in November, 30 cm (12 in) from the base

Graft

In February or March prune the secondary stems of climbing roses above two buds

Ramblers, ground-cover, climbing and remontant roses

As the grower will have already reduced them in height by 50 cm (20 in) for planting out, you won't need to prune these roses in the first year. In subsequent years simply choose the four or five stems that you wish to retain and remove the rest. For climbing roses, training ensures that all the branches are inclined towards your chosen support. In the following years continue to guide and gently direct the branches to slow their growth and encourage flowering. From the fourth winter onwards, remove the two or three oldest primary branches at the base of the plant.

Dwarf cluster-flowered roses, shrub roses, standards and half-standards

Maintain a uniform, vigorous growth on the four outside branches of the plant by pruning above the second or third bud, counted from the collar of the plant. Remove the weakest branches at their base. In the following years prune regularly to rejuvenate.

Weeping or umbrella remontant roses

In contrast to other roses, prune the branches above a bud situated on the inside of the stem.

Climbers, non-remontants and weeping roses

As these roses flower only once during the summer, light pruning is carried out when flowering has finished remove any diseased or twiggy growth.

Fruit trees: planting, pruning ...

The aim of pruning is not just to encourage the formation of fruit – unpruned trees still blossom and bear fruit – but to encourage better quality fruit and to prevent disease.

Pruning to encourage a high yield

Pruning during and after the fruit-forming period encourages fruiting. Primary pruning – carried out in winter – triggers new growth. Vigorous growth should be pruned lightly, thinning out some shoots completely and leaving a percentage unpruned. Horizontal branches tend to be more fruitful than vertical ones. Tie some vertical laterals down towards the horizontal to encourage fruiting.

Planting

If it's presented in bare-root form, the fruit tree should be planted between November and March, when it is dormant. Plant the tree in a mixture of soil and organic matter, such as well-rotted manure or compost. This will encourage rootlets to emerge, encouraging vigorous growth. If you buy a container-grown tree, you will have more time to plant it, but avoid frosty periods.

Pruning at the time of planting

When first removed from the nursery, the root system of a container-grown tree is restricted. It is essential to reduce the upper portion of the tree to limit water loss through the foliage. Fruits with pips, such as apples and pears, revive more readily and do not require such hard pruning as stone fruits.

Pruning to create an attractive shape

Initial pruning on a young tree consists of removing unwanted shoots and shortening those to be retained only if necessary. This process continues during the first two or three years, until the desired shape has been achieved.

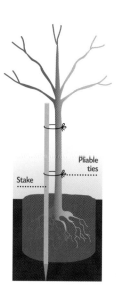

Stake

Pliable ties

HARD PRUNING OF A STONE FRUIT

Cut two-thirds off the end of each shoot

TAPERED PRUNING FOR FRUIT FORMATION

Treat wounds caused by pruning with Stockholm tar or **grafting wax**

...and grafting

Fruit trees are usually propagated by grafting, which is most successfully carried out in midsummer. A bud from the plant is cut from a ripe shoot of the current season's growth. The shoot should be vigorous, approximately pencil thick and have well-developed buds. It is then grafted onto an incision made in the stem of the rootstock plant. The rootstock provides the root system that will feed the new plant, while the scion determines its species and variety. The appearance of the tree and its fruits are therefore determined by the scion.

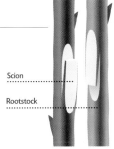

Scion

Rootstock

Propagation by T-budding

This is the most popular method for propagating fruit trees. Choose vigorous shoots of the current season's ripened wood for the scions. Make a T-shaped slit in the bark of the rootstock and lift it off on just one side of the slit. Slide the scion under the flap of bark. Bind right up to the top of the graft with transparent grafting tape.

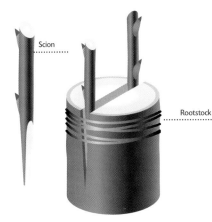

Scion

Rootstock

The cleft graft

Split the rootstock at its centre, keeping it open with the aid of a wedge. Prepare two scions, choosing semi-ripe shoots with three to four buds. Strip the bark from one side of each scion and then slide a scion into each end of the cut in the rootstock. Bind together and cover the graft with grafting wax.

Scion

Rootstock

Propagation by rind grafting

The tree is prepared in mid-spring by cutting back most of the main branches. The scions should be pencil-thick ripened shoots of the previous season's growth. They are cut into sections. Long, straight cuts are then made through the bark of the stock tree. A scion is inserted into each cut and bound with grafting tape.

Propagation by cuttings...

As well as the division of rootstock and grafting, plants may be propagated using cuttings or by layering. In both cases root growth is stimulated on a portion of the plant. Propagation by cuttings consists of cutting off stems, roots or leaves from the parent plant, and encouraging the appearance of roots, thus generating an independent new plant.

Propagation of cuttings in water

Few cuttings from outdoor plants regenerate in water, with the exception of fuchsias, pelargoniums and oleanders. Immerse the stem only, not the leaves. Once roots have appeared, don't wait too long before you pot up the cutting because there aren't enough nutrients in the water to keep the new plant alive for long.

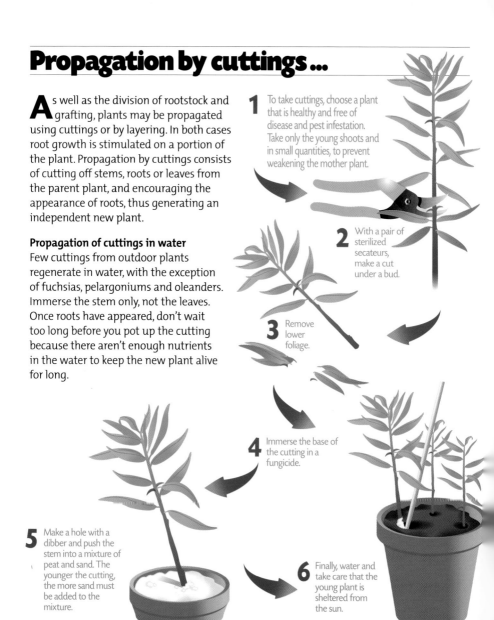

1 To take cuttings, choose a plant that is healthy and free of disease and pest infestation. Take only the young shoots and in small quantities, to prevent weakening the mother plant.

2 With a pair of sterilized secateurs, make a cut under a bud.

3 Remove lower foliage.

4 Immerse the base of the cutting in a fungicide.

5 Make a hole with a dibber and push the stem into a mixture of peat and sand. The younger the cutting, the more sand must be added to the mixture.

6 Finally, water and take care that the young plant is sheltered from the sun.

... and layering

Layering consists of inducing a shoot to root while it is still attached to the parent plant. Select a strong, healthy shoot and thoroughly cultivate the ground around it. Peg down the shoot to the ground, securing it loosely to allow for new growth. Fill in the area around it with a mixture of soil and cutting compost. Keep the layers watered during the summer.

When to layer

Carry out layering from mid-autumn to early spring. Separate the rooted layer from the parent plant in autumn, when the shoots will be vigorous.

When to take cuttings

There are two distinct periods for propagation by cuttings: from March to May for perennials and from mid-August to the end of September for shrubs and conifers, because this corresponds to the time when the young tissues become woody before winter.

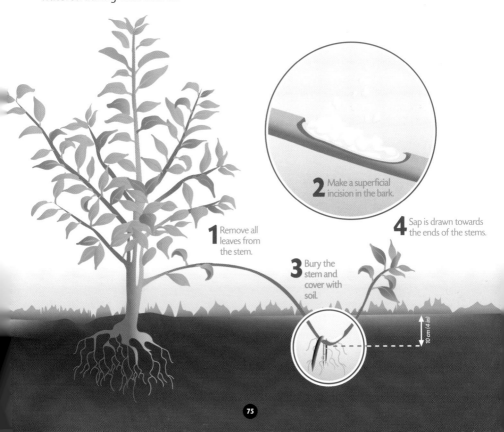

2 Make a superficial incision in the bark.

1 Remove all leaves from the stem.

4 Sap is drawn towards the ends of the stems.

3 Bury the stem and cover with soil.

10 cm (4 in)

The lawn

The lawn is sown with a mixture of grass varieties, chosen to create a perfect combination. Choose your seed mix to suit your soil and your own needs. Follow these three simple rules – sow generously, feed well and water sufficiently – and you will create a beautiful carpet of grass. A beautiful lawn depends on maintenance.

Dry soils

In areas exposed to full sun, choose a mixture of fine-leaved fescues and a little perennial ryegrass to ensure rapid coverage. This mixture tolerates some water shortage and adapts well to poor soil.

A playground

A mixture with a base of well-rooted meadow grass and fast-growing perennial ryegrass, red fescue and fine-leaved reed fescue is ideal for playgrounds. It is hard-wearing and will grow back well.

The bowling green lawn

The 'formal' lawn, typical of many English gardens, is composed of delicate grass species, which will not tolerate difficult climatic conditions and will demand constant maintenance. The basis of this lawn is a mixture of fine-leaved fescues (*Festuca rubra* var. *commutata* and *F. r.* var. *rubra*) and browntop and highland bent (*Agrostis tenuis* and *A. castellana*), greedy for both water and fertiliser. Mown very short, it gives a sumptuous velvety effect. If you prefer a wild garden, choose a mixture with flowers (cornflower, poppy, daisy), which needs only one mow in late summer.

Using turf

Supplied as a roll, you unroll the turf on to soil that has been prepared by turning and weeding. Ten days later, you'll have a lawn that has rooted sufficiently to be walked on. The best time to lay turf is between October and March.

SCARIFYING YOUR LAWN

In spring and autumn rake the length and then the width of the lawn. Gather up the waste material, spread a little sand over the lawn, then water. Finish this rejuvenating treatment by applying some fertiliser.

WHEN TO SOW?

Sow from April to May or in October, when the soil is still warm.

LAWN MAINTENANCE

Aerate your lawn at least once a year using a spiked roller or a gardening fork.

LAWN REPAIRS

To replace a damaged part of your lawn, cut out the damaged patch, turn it over and reseed.

1 After first applying a weed killer, dig over the soil to a depth of 20 cm (8 in).

2 Remove any stones from the soil, then rake the surface.

3 If you wish, level the ground to provide a flat surface.

4 With the aid of a seed bag, scatter the mixture at a rate of 30 g (1 oz) of seed per square metre (1 square yard). To ensure that the seed is evenly spread, walk across the area twice in opposite directions.

5 Rake lightly to incorporate the seed.

6 Water, preferably in the evenings, to avoid evaporation. Water thoroughly but not too frequently, to encourage root development.

7 Apply a specialist lawn fertiliser, rich in nitrogen, and always spread it on moist soil so as not to burn the shoots.

A calendar for garden maintenance

MARCH

Roses: Prune **remontant** roses; finish planting bare-root roses; hoeing around their bases and making sure that they're not infested with aphids.

Plants and shrubs: Prune hedges. Plant climbers (honeysuckle, clematis, Virginia creeper, passion flower), perennial foliage plants (viburnum, spindle-tree, box, Mexican orange blossom) and those requiring acid soil (rhododendron, magnolia, heather). In most regions, plants protected from frost c be uncovered.

Lawn: Scarify, aerate a spread fertiliser.

JANUARY

Roses: Treat against hibernating species of harmful pests.

Plants and shrubs: After any snowfall, shake the branches of evergreen shrubs so they don't break under the weight.

Lawn: Avoid walking on the lawn if it's frozen or covered in snow.

FEBRUARY

Roses: Prune at the end of the month. Spread some rose fertiliser and apply selective weed killer around the base.

Plants and shrubs: Begin pruning the summer-flowering shrubs, if it doesn't freeze. Spread weed killer on the paths.

Lawn: Treat with a chemical moss killer and then remove by scarifying the lawn.

DECEMBER

Roses: Begin planting. Earth up the rose bushes.

Plants and shrubs: Create new borders. Continue planting out trees and shrubs. Remove any dead branches.

Lawn: Do not walk on frozen or waterlogged lawns.

NOVEMBER

Roses: Prepare the beds.

Plants and shrubs: Cover delicate plants. Prune evergreen hedges. Dig over flowerbeds. Plant bare-root species.

Lawn: Sweep up dead leaves.

OCTOBER

Roses: Dead-head. Plant.

Plants and shrubs: Begin winter jobs, wherever possible. Plant conifers, trees, shrubs. Finish pruning the hedges. Mulch the perennials.

Lawn: Mow until the first frosts.

APRIL

Roses: Spread fertiliser and rake the surrounding soil. Remove suckers below the grafting point.
Plants and shrubs: Plant summer-flowering bulbs (gladioli, lily) and autumn-flowering bulbs (dahlia); plant out conifers and shrubs.

Begin sowing biennials, and the perennials such as columbine, foxgloves, carnations or perennial poppies. Thin young seedlings from the annuals.
Lawn: Sow any new grass seed; begin mowing and watering the existing lawns again.

MAY

Roses: Water, taking care not to wet the leaves if the weather is dry. After the first flowering, dead-head.
Plants and shrubs: Plant all summer flowers (geraniums, salvias, petunias); sow annuals in open soil and prick out the biennials. Mulch recently planted

flowerbeds. Dead-head shrubs. Prune any climbers that have substantially grown (ivy, Virginia creeper).
Lawn: Mow at least every 10 days. Still an appropriate time for planting grass seed. Water profusely in the evening or at night if necessary.

JUNE

Roses: Remove dead flowerheads. Keep an eye out for pests and diseases. Water and spread fertiliser liberally.
Plants and shrubs: Put in aquatic plants; prune conifer hedges and any shrubs that have finished flowering (lilac, forsythia). At the end of the month, remove

spring bulbs if wished, as their foliage will have turned very yellow. Hoe shrub beds regularly to aerate and remove weeds. Plant the last perennial seeds; water trees and shrubs planted at the beginning of the year or in the previous autumn profusely. Last sowing of annuals.

SEPTEMBER

Roses: Prune back the remontant varieties, which won't flower again.
Plants and shrubs: Finish pricking out biennials (wallflowers, pansies etc.). Take cuttings from the conifers. Remove dead heads, prepare and hoe the soil. Feed perennials with humus, peat and compost.
Lawn: Remove weeds.

AUGUST

Roses: Water remontant roses and feed with fertiliser. Treat against mildew and aphids.
Plants and shrubs: Take cuttings from pelargoniums and acid-loving plants. Apply weed killer to rockeries. Mulch climbing shrubs. Stake perennials. Prick out biennials.
Lawn: Prepare the soil for future sowings.

JULY

Roses: Remove dead blooms. Keep an eye out for diseases and insects.
Plants and shrubs: Divide perennial plants. Sow spring biennials (pansies, forget-me-nots). Remove faded flowers from borders.
Lawn: Mow and water frequently if the weather is hot, but don't apply any fertiliser or weed killer.

Over-wintering horticultural fleece, held up by an arch

Straw barrier

Bubble wrap

Mulch

Protecting your plants

The natural protection of mulches

A mulch is a top-dressing, usually of a bulky, organic material. Mulching keeps the soil moist and at the same time protects against a sudden drop in temperature. An old and natural technique, it also makes the gardener's task easier by suppressing weeds. Spread the mulch thickly over a weed-free soil, making sure that it does not sink, and hoe regularly with a claw hoe, especially after heavy rain. There are many materials that can serve as mulches that can be found in most garden centres – peat, bark, manure, coir or coconut fibre, gravel, straw or compost. However, be sure to use them with care. Bark, which is by nature acid, is better suited to the mulching of rhododendrons or azaleas. For alpine or rockery plants, choose fine gravel, and for the base of trees and shrubs use straw or hay. Coir or coconut fibre is spread around perennial plants and beds. In the vegetable garden, leaf mould is spread on seed and herb beds.

Winter protection

A bove all, identify the plants in your garden or balcony that are sensitive to frost. The best time to install winter protection is from the end of November to the first weeks in December. Don't take protective measures too early because the plants need to cool down in order to slow their growth in preparation for winter. The following types of protection will serve to diminish the intensity of frost and to maintain the plants in the driest atmosphere possible, because a thaw can be just as dangerous as the frost. If it thaws out too quickly, a plant may die.

Horticultural fleece

Non-woven, horticultural fleece can be used to protect plants and pots against frost. Permeable to water and air, it allows light to filter through. This light is essential to perennial plants, which must be allowed to continue their cycle. It's fixed by means of a frame around pruned shrubs with deciduous foliage to form a hood over plants that are sensitive to frost, such as camellias; or it is draped over climbers and espalier fruit trees.

Bubble wrap

An effective winter coat, the material must never come into direct contact with the plant. It should be fastened on to a light frame placed around the plant. Be prepared to aerate to avoid harmful condensation forming on sunny days.

Garden hessian

Garden hessian is sold by the metre and is used to cover small pots.

The organic garden

Intensive use of chemical products often proves harmful. Achieving an organic balance has again become a priority. Gardeners' control is reduced to a minimum and they must accept that nature can thrive without them.

Basic principles

Planning organic growing methods for your garden is a long-term process that requires total commitment. Cultivate the soil so that it feeds the vegetables and flowers more efficiently. Sometimes it is better to use the 'no-dig' system, allowing the micro-organisms to break down the organic matter in the soil naturally. Feed the soil with green manures, which will improve and maintain the structure and fertility of the soil. Plan crop rotation, especially in the vegetable garden, combining plants that naturally protect each other. Create an environment where beneficial insects can thrive, and be aware that pests cannot be entirely eliminated: you can only hope to reduce the damage that they cause. Finally, plant species that will attract birds and pollen- and nectar-producing plants that will attract useful insects to the garden. These are some of the many simple measures within the scope of every gardener.

GREEN MANURES

Manures are very beneficial in the domestic vegetable garden. They are leguminous plants that have notrigen-fixing root nodules (clover, alfalfa, buckwheat, lupin or mustard), and liquid fertiliser made from an infusion of weeds such as comfrey or seaweed.

Incorporating green manure

Ground must lie fallow for two or three months before green manure can be dug into it. Some fertilisers should be used before winter, others in spring.

After trimming, allow the cuttings to dry

Incorporate them into the soil by turning over the earth

Comfrey liquid manure

This is obtained by steeping comfrey leaves in water for three weeks. The juice recovered through straining and pressing is ready for immediate use.

Make a hole of about 5 cm (2 in) wide in the bottom of the drum

Once the liquid has been drained, keep the container in the shade, away from light and cold

Compost

Plants require nitrogen, phosphoric acid and potash for healthy growth – elements that are naturally present in compost. The summer heat encourages bacterial life and fermentation in the compost heap. As a result, the temperature rises to between 50°C and 60°C in the centre of the heap and the compost takes only three months to make during the summer months. During the cold winter months it can take five months or more.

If the compost doesn't warm up, water generously and add an activator such as manure or grass clippings.

You'll get 500 g (15 oz) of compost from 5 kg (11 lbs) of waste.

How to make compost

Choose a sunny spot. Place the waste (dead leaves, straw, vegetable peelings, manure, paper or cardboard and grass cuttings) in regular 20 cm (8 in) layers, with a layer of earth between each one. The following should never be put on the heap: inorganic waste (glass, metal, plastic), detergents and chemical products, colour magazines, treated weeds, and fallen leaves, which rot down too slowly. The compost heap should contain products that rot down at the same rate. Water each layer, making sure the heap is moist but not flooded. In winter, after applying some activator, cover over the top

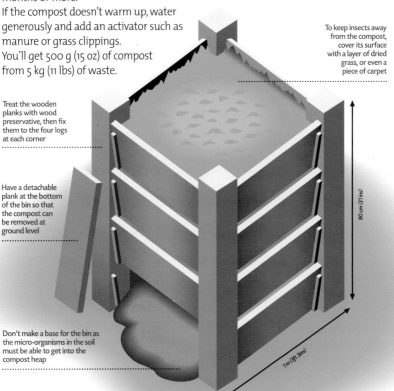

To keep insects away from the compost, cover its surface with a layer of dried grass, or even a piece of carpet

Treat the wooden planks with wood preservative, then fix them to the four logs at each corner

Have a detachable plank at the bottom of the bin so that the compost can be removed at ground level

Don't make a base for the bin as the micro-organisms in the soil must be able to get into the compost heap

80 cm (31 ins)

1 m (3ft 3ins)

Defend your garden

The garden has its enemies – there are many pests and diseases. Learn to identify the attacking insect or disease so that you can provide the appropriate treatment for your plants.

Insects

It's natural to find insects in a garden. Birds and ladybirds busy themselves with maintaining the biological balance, but we still need to prevent the garden from being overrun.

A harmful insect is easy to spot, living in colonies along the stems or on the leaves. This is a certain sign of an infestation by aphids, bugs or mites.

Signs of disease

Misshapen, shrivelled, mottled, curled or discoloured leaves are a sign of disease. Pits or small holes in the leaves signal the presence of slugs, caterpillars or flea beetles. Shoots are a good indicator in the vegetable garden. Eaten, brown or discoloured patches indicate the presence of destructive insects such as aphids, vine weevils and cutworm.

Pelargonium leaf gall (bacterial leaf spots)

Mildew

Rust

PREVENTING DISEASE
Bordeaux mixture, tar oil.

Aphids

Flea beetles

Whiteflies

Fruit trees and conifers

Protecting fruit trees and conifers begins
with a generally high level of hygiene. Burn
any diseased or infested branches and keep
an eye on the tree's bark and shoots. Red
spots, thick discharges or white patches
indicate an infection that should be treated.
Even if the garden is healthy, you can still
observe preventive measures. By spraying
against potential pests every fortnight, from
the beginning of spring to the end of
summer, you may prevent the appearance
of the destructive pest or the spread of
disease.

Diseases in the vegetable garden

There are two common categories: parasitic
diseases, such as mildew and rust, or viral
diseases, such as potato blight, mosaic
disease and leaf curl. Protecting your
vegetable garden requires some preventive
measures – removing weeds, burning
infested seeds and plants. Choose resistant
varieties and seeds and control your crop
production – excessive fertiliser, too much
water and sowing seeds too densely can
weaken your plants and encourage infection
to take hold.

Treatment

For both insects and
diseases removing and
burning the infested
leaves may suffice. If the
disease continues to
spread, treatment is
required. There are
pesticides appropriate
for any situation:
insecticides treat
infestation by insects;
fungicides treat fungal
infections; acaricides,
such as malathion,
exterminate spider
mites. Some of these
products are mixed,
which enables you to
combat several enemies
at once. Give priority to
selective products
developed to destroy a
specific pest or disease,
while respecting the rest
of the garden.

TREES AND LAWN

Don't just water for a short period because water must soak into the soil over a considerable time, allowing the lawn's roots to develop. Water a large shrub or tree around the base covering the whole area corresponding to its foliage. Watering at the base of the trunk is insufficient. For beds and hedges optimise the effect of each watering by spreading a mulch at the base of the plants. It will store water and lessen evaporation.

Outside tap for easy access

Hose, long enough to stretch across the whole garden

Watering can

Rainwater butt, economical and good for plants

Nozzle

Chrysanthemums are the first to suffer when there's a shortage of water, evident by the appearance of dry and wilting leaves.

Drain collecting used water

Watering

As a rule, water in the morning in autumn, winter and spring, the seasons that are prone to temperature drops at night. In summer water in the evening, for a long time, as this will reduce the evaporation caused by heat and avoid scorching due to drops of water forming magnifying glasses that reflect the sun's rays. In the vegetable garden and the orchard over-watering encourages parasites and produces watery vegetables and tasteless fruit.

The vegetable garden

Water requirements are aproximately 6 litres (10 pints) a day per square metre (square yard), which is about 40 litres (70 pints) per square metre (square yard) per week. Water the roots directly to avoid waste. If the soil is covered with a mulch, limit watering to every 10 to 15 days. Reduce watering a month before lifting the vegetables as excessive water can cause rotting.

Economical drip-feed irrigation system, giving the exact volume of water required for the vegetable garden, hedges and beds

Underground rotating sprinkler

Perforated hosepipe is deal for large areas

The flowering calendar

November and December
Ornamental cabbage, chrysanthemum, pansy, cyclamen, nerine, Michaelmas daisy, fern, grasses, Christmas bamboo, heather, holly, rosemary, santolina, evergreen sage, vine, conifers and evergreens.

January
Ornamental cabbage, Christmas rose, periwinkle, bamboo, box, dogwood, witch-hazel, holly, jasmine, viburnum all conifers and evergreens. Salix bebyloniaca var. pekinensis 'Tortuosa'.

February
Ornamental cabbage, pansy, crocus, snowdrop, grape hyacinth, Christmas rose, daphne, ivy, mahonia, mimosa, pieris, cornelian cherry, hazel, willow.

March
Pasque flower, pansy, primrose, species narcissus, reticulate irises, Anemone blanda, cowslip, sweet violet, Fritillaria meleagris, camellia, evergreen clematis, daphne, forsythia, skimmia, poplar, flowering cherry.

April
Wallflower, forget-me-not, pansy, primrose, campion, chionodoxa, cyclamen, erythronium, grape hyacinth, hyacinth, tulip, columbine, daffodil, yellow alyssum, hawkweed, dwarf iris, dwarf dicentra, amelanchier, azalea, phlox, wisteria, viburnum, clematis, cherry, redcurrant, magnolia, rhododendron, apple blossom.

October

Ageratum, cobaea, autumn crocus, sunflower, marigold, zinnia, amaryllis, cyclamen, dahlia, nerine, helichrysum, Japanese anemone, Michaelmas daisy, gentian, pampas grass, heather, callicarpa, evergreen berries, ginkgo, larch, service tree, sumach, tulip tree.

September

Amaranthus, busy lizzie, China aster, sunflower, verbena, zinnia, autumn crocus, cyclamen, dahlia, gaura, grasses, gypsophila, phlox, heather, hydrangea, St John's wort, rose, shrub veronica, Japanese maple, service tree.

August

Begonia, coleus, cosmos, fuchsia, French marigold, petunia, sweet pea, African marigold, sunflower, zinnia, canna indica, dahlia, gladioli, gloriosa, lily, aster, grasses, gypsophila, heliopsis, bergamot, carnation, phlox, buddleia, hydrangea, lavender, potentilla, summer tamarisk, laburnum, sophora.

July

Cornflower, nasturtium, clarkia, poppy, foxglove, fuchsia, geranium, lobelia, acidanthera, agapanthus, lily, tuberous begonia, lily, oxalis, acanthus, arum lily, achillea, aster, campanula, eryngium, delphinium, gaillardia, helenium, lupin, phlox, scabious, bignonia, ceanothus, hibiscus, hydrangea, lavender, passion flower, remontant rose, summer spiraea, laburnum, sapindus, sophora.

June

Anthemis, foxglove, gazania, sweet William, allium, anemone, lily, arum, eremurus, lily, ranunculus, alchemilla, borage, iris, rock rose day lily, loosestrife, carnation, poppy, periwinkle, primrose, pyrethrum, honeysuckle, cistus, large-flowered clematis, single-flowering and old garden roses, escallonia, St John's wort, shrub veronica, catalpa, tamarisk.

May

Wallflower, Iceland poppy, pansy, ornamental garlic, freesia, fritillary, lily-of-the-valley, ranunculus, tulip, columbine, dwarf aster, geum, campanula, geranium, iris, wild pink, peony, Judas tree, azalea, ceanothus, small-flowered clematis, laburnum, broom, lilac, Mexican orange, rhododendron, mock orange, hawthorn, paulownia, robinia, sorbus.

Balconies, roof gardens and patios

By providing a green environment, a balcony can become an oasis for passionate gardeners living in the city. However, the climatic conditions on balconies and roof gardens – which can include strong wind and intense sun – are not ideal for growing plants in pots.

Trellises and pergolas

These structures make excellent windbreaks, and can also be used to disguise unattractive fences, dividing walls or even undesirable views from balconies and terraces. Trellises support climbing plants and can also be used to grow shrubs or fruit trees as espaliers. Available in panels of various sizes, choose the trellis according to the site and the amount of privacy that you desire, bearing in mind the nature of the creeper or climbing plant that it will eventually support. Always choose a good quality trellis in treated wood as this will not rot and maintenance will be minimal – repairing a trellis is difficult once it is covered in a climbing plant.

Once assembled, these trellis screens and pergolas not only provide plants with a structure they can cling to but also create an invaluable area of shade.

Balcony containers

Without careful planning and thought, balcony containers can often look dull. This can be the result not only of their planting but also of their arrangement on the terrace or balcony. To achieve contrast, plant species of varying heights and colours in a large container or group different sized pots together to create a pleasing effect. Choose good quality pots in either PVC or fibreglass. Other materials may be even lighter, but remember that poor quality pots can lose their shape under the weight of the potting compost. For safety, choose pots with brackets so that they can be fixed to a wall or railing.

Terracotta pots

The porous structure of terracotta allows air to penetrate the pot. This is beneficial to the roots of the plant, but on the other hand, you do need to water more frequently. Avoid buying a pot without drainage holes, as you risk breaking it when you make the hole yourself. Less resistant to frost than wooden or resin tubs, terracotta pots should be as thick as possible. Hand-made pots will cost more, but their quality will be superior to that of mass-produced ones.

Hanging baskets

Accommodating both simple summer flowers (petunias, impatiens, tobacco plants), and trailing or cascading plants, such as ivy or lobelia, hanging baskets don't have to be positioned at eye level. Select a site to suit the plants that you have chosen. The main disadvantage of hanging baskets is that they are sometimes difficult to water. Make sure that water loss is kept to a minimum by lining them with sphagnum moss or clay. If plastic-coated felt covers are not supplied with metal baskets, you can line them yourself to two-thirds of their height with a film of black plastic, pierced with a few holes for drainage. Incorporate a bed of fine gravel to act as ballast and drainage at the base, before filling them with peat substitute.

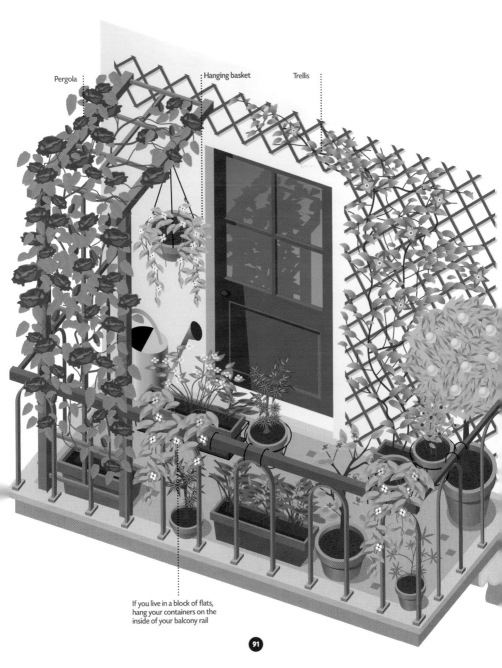

Pergola

Hanging basket

Trellis

If you live in a block of flats, hang your containers on the inside of your balcony rail

Design your own vegetable garden

Watching your own vegetables grow and then harvesting them gives the deepest satisfaction to any gardener. The vegetable garden is a feast in every sense of the word – there is nothing quite like the taste of fresh, home-grown vegetables.

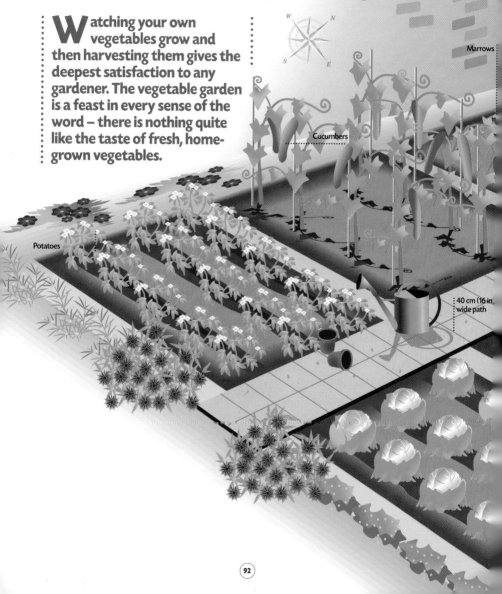

Marrows

Cucumbers

Potatoes

40 cm (16 in.) wide path

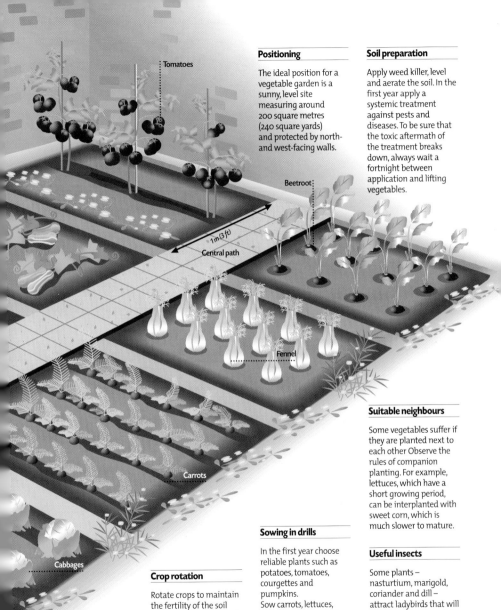

Tomatoes

Beetroot

1 m (3 ft)

Central path

Fennel

Carrots

Cabbages

Positioning

The ideal position for a vegetable garden is a sunny, level site measuring around 200 square metres (240 square yards) and protected by north- and west-facing walls.

Soil preparation

Apply weed killer, level and aerate the soil. In the first year apply a systemic treatment against pests and diseases. To be sure that the toxic aftermath of the treatment breaks down, always wait a fortnight between application and lifting vegetables.

Suitable neighbours

Some vegetables suffer if they are planted next to each other Observe the rules of companion planting. For example, lettuces, which have a short growing period, can be interplanted with sweet corn, which is much slower to mature.

Sowing in drills

In the first year choose reliable plants such as potatoes, tomatoes, courgettes and pumpkins. Sow carrots, lettuces, onions and beans in the second year.

Useful insects

Some plants – nasturtium, marigold, coriander and dill – attract ladybirds that will rid your plot of harmful insects like aphids.

Crop rotation

Rotate crops to maintain the fertility of the soil and minimise the risk of viral cross-infection.

The vegetable calendar

JANUARY

Order your seeds. In mild weather, aerate by digging over the loose soil. Lay out your vegetable garden, spread manure. Pick the Brussels sprouts, winter leeks and lamb's lettuce. Sow lettuces, cabbages and leeks under cold frames.

FEBRUARY

Dig over the loose soil. Divide clumps of rhubarb, mint and tarragon. Lift and divide and position spring onion, chives and sorrel. Plant prepared potatoes. Plant garlic, onions and shallots. Sow carrots and radishes, broad beans, turnips and the first peas under cold frames.

MARCH

Plant aromatic frost-resistant species: rosemary, rhubarb, bay and thyme. Sow salads, cabbages, parsley, basil, leeks, tomatoes, courgettes and melons under cold frames. Eradicate slugs and snails. Sow carrots, radishes, peas, beans, broad beans, beetroot and spinach.

JULY

Pick herbs. Hoe the soil. Lift vegetables, water the base of plants in the evening. Sow for autumn: cabbages and salads. Plant out cabbages that germinated in June, and summer lettuces. pinch out side shoots of tomatoes. Sow beetroot, curly endive, turnips, leeks and beans up to the middle of the month. Sow parsley. Mulch soil.

AUGUST

Prick out the previous month's seedlings. Sow lamb's lettuce and winter salads. Spread fertiliser. Pick shallots, onions, and garlic. Blanch salads and celery. Continue sowing lamb's lettuce and turnips for winter. At the end of the month sow white onions and winter spinach. Plant new salads and leeks for winter.

SEPTEMBER

Protect salad vegetables from the cold. Sow turnips, cabbage, onions, leeks, white and red onions, lamb's lettuce, sorrel, spinach and radish under cold frames. Blanch celery plants by binding and earthing up the stalks. Plant winter curly endive. Cut the stems and leaves from your root vegetables and thin out tomatoes and aubergines to accelerate ripening.

APRIL

Prick out the seedlings in seed trays. Sow tomatoes, courgettes, melons, basil, salad vegetables, aubergines, peppers and cucumbers under cold frames. Sow broad beans, beetroot, Swiss chard, cabbages, spinach, onions and radishes in open ground. Earth up potatoes.

MAY

Prick out the plants raised under cold frames. Hoe the soil. Sow the beans in drills. Thin out seedlings. Once the frosts are over, sow French bean seeds, leeks, autumn salad vegetables and cabbages. Plant the last potatoes for lifting from September to October.

JUNE

Sow radishes at fortnightly intervals, making sure that you water them regularly. Sow salad beetroots for lifting in October, celery and celeriac, curly endive, winter carrots, Brussels sprouts and cabbages. Lift aromatic plants. Mulch the soil. Train runner (tomatoes, beans).

OCTOBER

Lift the remaining vegetables: tomatoes, marrows and pumpkins and finish ripening them inside. Store root vegetables. Plant strawberry plants in the second half of the month and keep well protected. In healthy, well-drained soil, plant garlic, shallots, winter salad vegetables, carrots, beetroots, radish and turnips. Break up the soil.

NOVEMBER

Prolong harvest by covering the last vegetables with a cloche. Mulch the soil at the base of rhubarb, leeks and celery. Last chance to plant garlic and strawberry plants. Earth up the artichokes. Begin winter jobs. Enrich the soil with compost or fertiliser. Place chervil, parsley and sorrel under a cold frame.

DECEMBER

Protect tender plants with horticultural fleece. In the event of a hard frost, double the protection. Pick lamb's lettuce, carrots, celery and Jerusalem artichokes. Dig over the loose soil in large spadefuls and spread manure over the ground.

The strawberry plant

Strawberries or raspberries are a must for any gardener who enjoys growing fruit and vegetables. If you have the space, buy about 50 plants – 25 perpetual and 25 early or midsummer varieties.

Make your choice

The good early and midsummer varieties are: 'Honeoye', which bears a heavy crop; 'Royal Sovereign', which has an excellent flavour; and 'Elsanta', which has firm, attractive berries. The good perpetual varieties are: 'Mara des bois', which combines the flavour of a wild strawberry with the size of cultivated fruit and 'Marastil', which produces good-sized fruit over a very long period.

Planting

Plant out strawberries immediately. Enrich the soil with manure – one full wheelbarrow per 10 cubic metres (13 cubic yards) should suffice. Space strawberries at 45 cm (18 in) intervals in slightly raised rows, planted with the base of the crown at soil level.
In heavy soil incorporate sand or grit to improve drainage.

CARE

Spread a generous amount of compost around the plants and only water in the morning. From the end of flowering, spread a mulch around the base of each plant. In summer, fertilise, using a fertiliser rich in potash. Cut the surplus runners (between June and September) and hold the plants in the ground with the aid of fine wire. For plentiful yields, replace a proportion of the plants every year.

QUALITY

When buying, check the plants, not just the leaves. The crown should be in good condition.

FIND OUT

BEFORE BEGINNING ANY WORK IN THE GARDEN IT'S BEST TO GET TO KNOW YOUR SITE – ITS SOIL, CLIMATE AND ASPECT – AND TO BE UP TO DATE WITH ANY LEGISLATION RELATING TO GARDEN STRUCTURES THAT YOU MIGHT WANT TO BUILD. WE HAVE INCLUDED LISTS OF SYMPTOMS AND REMEDIES TO HELP YOU COMBAT DISEASES AND UNWANTED PESTS. AND FOR SHEER PLEASURE, THERE ARE SOME OLD RECIPES THAT WILL REAWAKEN YOUR TASTE BUDS TO THE DELIGHTS OF OLD, FORGOTTEN FLAVOURS.

Just like grandmother used to make

Artichoke au gratin

The globe artichoke is a spectacular sight in the vegetable garden and a delicious ingredient in the kitchen.

• Remove coarse outer scales and put into a pan of boiling water to which 2 tablespoonfuls of flour and lemon juice have been added. Simmer for 30 minutes.
• Drain the artichokes and brown them in a saucepan with 50 g (1 oz) of butter.
• Pour in 100 ml (5 fl. oz) of chicken stock, salt and pepper to taste and a pinch of nutmeg. Cook for 5 minutes.
• Heat the oven to gas mark 7 (220°C/425°F).
• Grease a gratin dish and pour in the mixture; sprinkling a layer of parmesan over the top.
• Brown for 20 minutes in the oven.

Aubergine 'caviar'

• Wrap whole aubergines in aluminium foil.
• Place them in a medium oven.
• Bake until tender, testing with a fork during cooking.
• Allow them to cool, then cut in two lengthways and remove the pulp.
• Mix the pulp with salt, pepper, lemon juice and olive oil until you have a thick paste.
• Serve on hot toast with a sprinkling of fresh basil .

Black potato with butter vinaigrette

This potato owes its name to the dark violet colour of its skin and flesh.

• Put 1 kg (2.2 lb) of black potatoes in salted water, bring to the boil and simmer for 20 minutes.
• Melt 25 g (1 oz) of butter, add 2 tablespoons of olive oil, 2 tablespoons of balsamic vinegar and salt and pepper.
• Remove from the heat, add 2 tablespoons of chopped parsley.
• Peel the potatoes, cut them lengthways and pour the sauce over them.
• Delicious with fried fish

A warm winter salad of Jerusalem artichokes

This is a delicious root vegetable from North America.
• Peel 800 g (11/2 lb) of Jerusalem artichokes, cut into slices and cook in salted water for 10 minutes.
• Prepare a vinaigrette with 1 tablespoon of balsamic vinegar, salt, pepper, and 4 tablespoons of olive oil.
• Drain the vegetables, pour the dressing over them and garnish with chives, chervil and lemon peel.

Courgette in a foil parcel

This courgette is cooked like other members of the marrow family, but it can also be used as a dessert.
• Wrap the courgette in aluminium foil and bake in a medium oven.
• Check whether it's cooked by pricking with a fork.
• Cut out the inside with a knife, sprinkle with sugar and add butter.

Parsnip vinaigrette

A member of the carrot family, parsnips have a unique, slightly sweet flavour.
• Peel and cut 1 kg (about 2 lb) of parsnips into pieces.
• Steam for 20 minutes.
• Prepare an olive oil and shallot vinaigrette and pour over the parsnips. Sprinkle with dill and serve warm.

Melon and fresh ginger syrup

• Cut a piece of root of ginger into fine strips.
• Cook ginger in a mixture of water and sugar until the liquid becomes a golden-coloured syrup.
• Cut the melons into two, remove and dice the flesh and mix it into the syrup.
• Serve chilled in the scooped out melon halves.

Wild spinach gnocchi

Squeeze 1 kg (about 2 lb) of fresh, cooked spinach dry between your hands and then chop very finely. Put the spinach in a bowl with 3 large eggs, 350 g (12 oz) ricotta cheese and 4 tablespoons of parmesan. Mix lightly and season with salt, pepper and 1/4 tsp of grated nutmeg. Add enough plain flour to thicken the mixture so that you can handle it easily. Shape the paste into 7.5 cm (3 in) croquette shapes and dust lightly with flour. Bring a large saucepan of salted water to the boil, add the gnocchi and cook for 1–2 minutes, or until they bob up to the surface. Put gnocchi in an oiled dish, sprinkle with grated gruyère cheese and brown under the grill.

Summer soup

• Heat 25 g (1 oz) butter and 1 tbs of oil in a large pan. Gently fry 1 chopped onion until soft. Add the outer leaves of a lettuce, 14 sorrel leaves and a handful of spinach. Simmer for 5 minutes and then add 50 g (2 oz) flour. Add 900 ml (11/2 pt) light stock, stirring until thickened. Simmer for 10 minutes. Purée and stir in 300 ml (1/2 pt) of milk and reheat. Serve with swirl of cream.

Chicken with chervil root

Chervil's aromatic flesh, reminiscent of the carrot, is a worthy addition to this recipe.
• Wash several chervil roots and put them into a saucepan with a little butter, 2 onions, 1 clove of garlic, 2 cloves, 1 bay leaf, thyme and basil.
• Cook over a medium heat until the colours run and moisten with 1 glass of white wine and 1 glass of stock.
• Over a gentle heat, reduce the liquid by half. Liquidise, adding a large knob of butter, a pinch of flour and chopped chervil to form a smooth sauce. Serve with roast chicken.

The soil and the climate

The soil supports your plants and acts as a vital source of nutrients. It is a living, ever-changing environment. Sand, silt, clay, limestone, water, air, humus and living organisms are its constituents, but to be fertile, soil must be balanced, which means having a structure that's capable of retaining and releasing nutritive elements.

To avoid expensive mistakes, find out what type of soil you have and plant the species that are best adapted to it. You can make a visual analysis of the soil type in your garden by removing a small amount of moist surface soil and rubbing it between your fingers. If it feels gritty and the grains don't stick together, then it's sandy soil; if it's sticky, compact and shiny, your soil is clay; silky and free-running soil is silty. If it's homogenous and compact without being heavy, your garden has healthy soil. A healthy soil with balanced mineral components combined with humus is considered the ideal. Aerated and well drained, it's the easiest to work and allows roots to become well established.

Acid or alkaline soil

Although many plants thrive in healthy soils or tolerate a small amount of acidity, some have strict requirements. To find out the measure of acidity or alkalinity (pH) of your soil, you can buy a test kit from a garden centre of hardware store. If the pH is number 7, your soil is neutral. Below 7 indicates an acid soil; above 7 indicates an alkaline soil. Depending on what the previous owner of your garden used it for, the pH can even vary from one area to the next. In that case, consider taking several soil samples. If you envisage planting fruit trees or plants that will remain in one spot for a long period, a more detailed analysis can prove useful, especially if you have drainage problems or an unsatisfactory pH level.

The fertility of the soil

The soil's fertility depends on how rich it is in nitrogen, phosphorus and potash, and you should, therefore, work to maintain these reserves which can become exhausted. Organic matter gradually disappears as the soil breaks down, and soil analysis can identify its deficiencies. Although organic manures incorporated into the soil will generally suffice, enriching agents are sometimes necessary. Applications of lime or potassium, both alkalines, effectively diminish the acidity of the soil, but they sometimes also diminish reserves of organic matter. Sand may be dug in to improve the structure of a heavy soil, such as clay. However, be aware that sand will also lower the pH level of an alkaline soil and must be incorporated in large quantities to be effective. As these soil improvers don't feed the plants, you'll need to add some fertiliser as well.

Judging the climate

Good gardeners know how important it is to take the local climate into account when they plan their garden. As attentive observers, they will already have seen how Mother Nature makes her own selection, distributing plants to the most suitable positions in the garden, according to their needs. The climate is at the core of everything that happens to the plants in your garden. Consequently, having green fingers is not enough, you need to allow for the rain, the sun and the wind, and plant according to their laws.

Micro-climates

In Britain we have a range of different micro-climates, depending on the latitude of the area in which we garden, the height of the garden above sea level and the proximity of the sea. Each area has a slightly different annual rainfall, wind speed and temperature range. All these factors must be considered in your choice of plants. It's vital to know whether your garden is prone to frost, in which case you should choose late-flowering plants.

Wind

Every plant's requirements for rain or sunshine are slightly different, but they are all sensitive to hail and wind. Wind accelerates the evaporation of water and restricts the plant's development. A garden situated in a windy zone will fare better with windbreaks or a screening of trees.

Altitude

In a hilltop garden, plants will be exposed to extreme temperatures. These are the conditions that only hardy plants will tolerate.

Aspect

A garden's aspect is another factor that must be considered. If it's north facing it will suit shade-loving plants; east-facing sites are for plants that prefer semi-shade; plants that can tolerate high humidity and strong winds are suitable for a west-facing garden; and a south-facing garden will suit plants which can tolerate full sun.

Treatments to use in your garden

PESTS	SUSCEPTIBLE PLANTS	SYMPTOMS	TREATMENT
Red spider mites	Strawberry plants, outdoor vines, figs, bulbs, vegetables, fruits, perennials, annuals	Mottled discoloration of leaves, which then yellow and drop off. Worst in greenhouses	Dimethoate, Malathion
Caterpillars	Brassicas	Holes in leaves	Remove by hand or spray with pyrethrum
Eelworms	Phlox, allium and onions	Leaves spotted with small, rough, yellow patches	Uproot and burn the affected plant
Chafer grubs	Young annuals, bulbs and vegetables	Large holes in root vegetables and bases of stems	Destroy larvae and water plants with pirimiphos methyl
Codling moth	Fruit trees	Holes tunnelled in ripe fruits	Hang pheromone traps in trees to trap male moths
Pea thrips	Peas	Pods turn silver-brown and remain flat	Spray with dimethoate
Hazel-nut weevil	Hazel-nut trees	Grubs that feed on nut kernels	HCH or permethrin
Pinebark aphid	Conifers	Aphids	Oleomalathion
Wireworms	Potatoes and other root crops	Tunnels bored into root crops	Pirimiphos-methyl
Swift moth caterpillars	Michaelmas daisy, phlox, peony, delphinium, chrysanthemum	Caterpillars	HCH or Pirimiphos-methyl
Leaf miner	Rosebushes, apple trees, shrubs, chrysanthemum	White or brown 'tunnels' within the leaf	HCH or Pirimiphos-methyl
Cutworm	Low-growing perennials, annuals, root vegetables and lettuces	Nibbled leaves and stems, caterpillars	Pirimiphos-methyl
Aphids	Rosebushes, fruit trees, vegetables	Colonies of insects	Malathion
Earwigs	Shrubs, perennials, annuals	Petals of flowers eaten in summer	Pirimiphos-methyl or HCH

DISEASE	SUSCEPTIBLE PLANTS	SYMPTOMS	TREATMENT
Anthracnose	Vegetable garden, fruit trees	Brown patches on the leaves	Copper, Mancozeb
Canker	Fruit trees, trees, shrubs	Brown patches towards the buds	Bordeaux mixture
Chlorosis	Rosebushes, pear trees, shrubs	Yellowing of the leaves	Trace elements
Leaf curl	Azaleas, peach trees	Leaves dropping and curling	Bordeaux mixture
Shothole	Chrysanthemums, carnations, bulbs, hyacinths	Decay	Bordeaux mixture
Fusarium wilt	Asters, runner beans	Red patches, leaves with necrosis	Burn effected plants
Strawberry leaf blotch	Rosebushes, strawberry plants	Discolouration of leaves	Systemic fungicide
Powdery mildew	Fruit trees, strawberries, vines, cucumbers, bulbs, herbaceous plants, roses.	Powdery mildew	Systemic fungicide
Spur canker	Fruit trees	Brown circular patches	Cut out effected area and apply canker paint
Downy mildew	Vines, seeds and seedlings, onions, leeks and parsnips	White mealy or furry growth	Mancozeb
Grey mould	Begonias, tulips, rosebushes, carnations, peonies, strawberry plants	Deterioration	Fungicide
Rust	Trees, shrubs, perennials.	Small bright orange patches.	Spray with mancozeb.

Gardening within your rights

Trees and boundaries

In both town and country, trees often mark the boundary between two properties. Problems can arise from this custom as it is not always clear which neighbour is responsible for the tree. Trees are not always mentioned in the deeds to a property and an 'unofficial' agreement may prove to be the only solution. Unfortunately, it's only when a tree begins to cause problems that anyone wonders who it belongs to. It may be that storm damage has resulted in a large quantity of timber that needs to be sawn up and cleared, or a branch may even have caused damage to a building. It's much better to resolve the question of the tree's ownership before such disasters occur. The roots of trees can cause damage to buildings belonging to you or your neighbour. Tree roots sometimes grow around drains, too, and though the root won't break a drain, if the pipe is leaky or cracked, it will certainly make it worse. If the problem becomes a matter for the insurance companies, you will find them keen to blame the nearest tree. They frequently ask for trees to be felled, even when the real cause of the problem is not clear.

Neighbours

The best thing you can do is to enquire at your local town council about your rights and restrictions before planting any trees. Generally speaking, everyone has the right to plant as many trees as they want in their own garden, even if they risk obscuring the view or cutting out light from their neighbours. Obviously, this is not recommended.

Highways and byways

Landowners – and that includes the owners of gardens – have a duty to keep roads or footpaths adjoining their property clear of vegetation. This means that plants and trees overhanging a road, pavement or footpath must be kept cut back. The local highways authority may do this on a routine basis for you, but they are not obliged to, and they may insist that you do the job yourself.

Noise

The use of lawnmowers, chain-saws and other kind of power-driven machinery are subject to bylaws that specify when they may be used. Enquire at your local council for details.

Construction

Even if you are erecting a structure that does not require planning permission, you would be wise to double check the legislation with the local planning office before commencing work.

Clearance and bonfires

In some areas there are restrictions regarding bonfires, and you should check these with your local council. Whenever possible, it makes much more sense to compost your garden waste.

Climbers

The wall up which you run your climbing plants, or against which you train your espalier trees may be a party wall or it may belong to you alone. Whatever the situation, try to ensure that your plants do not grow over the top of it. Your neighbour may consider you responsible if the plants damage the wall. The use of trellis panels, as discussed on page 90, may help to protect the wall from damage caused by climbers.

Fences, hedges, walls

Most gardens have some sort of boundary between them and neighbouring properties. In some cases the deeds of the house specify that there should be a boundary, often placing restrictions on its type and height. On new estates, the trend is towards open-plan front gardens. If you are planning to fence your plot, do check your deeds, as many specifically forbid the erection of any form of barrier in an open-plan setting.

Balconies and terraces

Before you embark on planning your balcony or terrace, do make sure that there are no restrictions on growing plants up the walls written into the deeds of your house or, if you are a tenant, the agreement with your landlord. The owners of rented property often take a negative attitude to tenants drilling holes in the wall to secure trellis or the brackets for pots or hanging baskets. Investigate all the regulations and restrictions carefully before you start. A roof terrace should always be surrounded by a guard-rail at least 1 metre (3 ft) high. If you are a tenant, be sure to ask for a signed authorisation from the property manager of your flat before making any significant improvements or alterations to your terrace or balcony. Bear in mind that some relatively small structures, such as greenhouses or sheds, are subject to planning permission.

'Monet's aim is to be intoxicated by the the air,
the light, the flowers and once again, the light.
With colour, he has unquestionably conquered
all things ephemeral that may be portrayed ...
He has captured all the different faces of
nature at every time of day ...'

A. Alexander
Le Figaro, December 1926

The gardens of the Impressionists

In western Europe, the 19th century was the period of the industrial revolution. Consequently, it was a time of radical change in the character and appearance of the landscape. Trapped in the industrial heart of the cities, the urban population began to yearn for the natural world that had been left behind. Many capitals, such as London and Paris, had railways. On Sundays the urban population streamed out into the countryside to walk and enjoy the fresh air.

Nature as a studio

It was in Île-de France and the Seine Valley that the Impressionists discovered the joy of painting the natural world. Painting pigments had only recently been packaged in tubes, which made it far easier to paint outside the studio. The name 'Impressionism' was initially a negative term, coined on the occasion of the first Impressionist exhibition in 1874. It was derived from a picture by Monet entitled *Impression, Sunrise*, painted by the artist as he was looked straight into the rising sun. The aim of the Impressionist movement was to achieve ever greater naturalism through an exact rendering of tone and colour and by closely observing the play of light on the surface of objects. The power of the sun was considered all important. Its rays lit up the world, enriching it with colour, producing transient snapshots of the landscape as the light moved and changed with the time of day. Each painter strove to preserve the spontaneity and freshness of the first impressions they captured, painting from life outdoors, and in their studios, too. It was the Impressionists' analysis of light and form that would eventually lead to the modern tradition of abstract painting.

Artists and gardeners

Of all the Impressionist painters, only Caillebotte, Pissarro and Monet had country gardens of their own. Their passion for gardening was as strong as their love of painting. It was another way of forming their own worlds, like those that they created on the painted canvas. Renoir was the only urban dweller, living in Paris with an uncultivated garden on Montmartre, while Pissarro gardened in the country at Éragny. Caillebotte had a garden at Petit Gennevilliers, and Monet moved from Argenteuil to Vétheuil, finally ending up at Giverny. Monet's last two gardens were brimming with horticultural content, becoming a real curiosity for botanists, with rare species of flowers and unusual colour combinations. The two artists corresponded about their gardens, and in his letters Caillebotte wrote about his rare roses and his orchids, while Monet discussed his irises and peonies, whose Japanese exoticism so inspired the Impressionists. 'Monet is only an eye, but what an eye, is how Cézanne described the foremost Impressionist among these painters and the most passionate gardener of his time. In 1883 Monet settled at Giverny, which was then a simple house with pink walls opening on to an orchard where apple trees grew exposed to the wind. He transformed the orchard into avenues of peonies, lilies, irises and foxgloves with the help of a head gardener and five assistants.

In 1893 he acquired a piece of marshy ground and dug out a pond where he planted yellow, white, red and mauve waterlilies, as well as a range of rare flowers sent by Tadamasa Hayashi, a Japanese merchant and collector. 'This garden at Giverny was a palette that Monet himself prepared. A yellow month – daffodils, orange blossom, nasturtium, all the golds of the earth revealed themselves to his eyes; the following month, with the wave of a wand, all the blues sprang up from his soil', J. des Gachons wrote in *Le National*.

The Thousand and One Nights, the thirty-sixth night

The garden – and what a garden! – opened on to a small arched door in the manner of a porch opening on to a large room and was festooned with vines bearing different types of grape, red like the hyacinth or black ebony. Visitors walked under an arbour where fruits were visible, set apart or in clusters; birds perched on the boughs and were singing all kinds of tunes; the nightingales continuously proclaimed their variations; the turtle-doves filled the void with their voices; the blackbirds had human tones; the wood pigeons appeared intoxicated. In pairs, the trees offered all kinds of fruits to taste, a little everywhere: camphor-apricots, almonds apricots from Khunrasan; plums that revealed the colour of beauty; cherries that give teeth their whiteness, figs that were half-red and half-white. There was also some orange blossom that was reminiscent of the pearl or the coral; the rose whose red offends the modest cheek of beautiful girls; the violet as radiant as sulphur ablaze in the night; myrtle, wallflower, lavender and anemone. The leaves were grazed with the tears from the clouds; the daisies were laughing like white teeth; the daffodil frequently glanced at the rose as a black man would; the citrons were reminiscent of goblets and the lemons of golden marbles. The ground was a carpet of flowers of a thousand shades; spring was manifest, it lit up all things with joy; the streams were mere murmurs, the birds only songs, the wind just a rustle, and the season simply a harmony.

Sunlight on the Lawn
Beverley Nichols

Oldfield, Merry Hall, the lilies – they were inseparable. The old man, the old house, the white flowers. I should never be able to think of the one without the other, for he had been standing by the regales on the first magic day – seven years ago, it was – when I crept through the deserted garden, a trespasser, little realising that this was to be my home for many happy years. It had been the sort of moment that must come to an explorer, when he has been plodding though a dark pass, and suddenly comes to a gap in the cliffs and sees, glittering before him, the snows of an uncharted mountain. I had fought my way through the weeds and brambles, towards an old brick wall, had found a gap in it and there, glittering before me, were the snows of the lilies. They really were sunlit now, and the fragrance as the breeze danced over them seemed to drift from the fields of heaven.

By them had been standing Oldfield, looking as old then as he did now. I shall always remember our first conversation. 'That's a wonderful lot of regales you've got there,' I had said. To which he had replied:

'Aye, they're pretty good,'

'Have they been established for long?'

'Thirty years or so.'

'Where did you get the bulbs?'

'Boolbs?' A snort. 'Boolbs? I didn't get boolbs. I grew 'em from a handful of seed.'

'Does that take long?'

'Three years. Of course, the garden book says seven. But I don't allus hold wi' garden books.'

The lilies were nearer forty years old now, except, of course, those which I had grown from seed myself. That had been one of our first jobs together, and sure enough, in three years they had flowered. Today, we had almost too many lilies.

Sunlight on the Lawn, 1956

The garden, a source of inspiration

GARDEN SONG

Here in this sequester'd close
Bloom the hyacinth and the rose,
Here beside the modest stock
Flaunts the flaring hollyhock;
Here, without a pang, one sees
Ranks, conditions and degrees.

All the seasons run their race
In this quiet resting-place;
Peach and apricot and fig
Here will ripen and grow big;
Here is store and overplus –
More had not Alcinoüs!

Here, in alleys cool and green,
Far ahead the thrush is seen;
Here along the southern wall
Keeps the bee his festival;
All is quiet else – afar
Sounds of toil and turmoil are.

Here be shadows large and long,
Here be spaces meet for song,
Grant, o garden-god, that I,
Now that none profane is nigh,–
Now that mood and moment please,–
Find the fair Pierides!

Henry Austin Dobson,
A Garden Song

TO AUTUMN

Season of mists and mellow fruitfulness!
Close bosom-friend of the maturing sun;
Conspiring with him how to load and bless
With fruit the vines that round the
thatch-eaves run;
To bend with apples the moss'd cottage trees,
And fill all fruit with ripeness to the core;
To swell the gourd, and plump
the hazel shells
With a sweet kernel; to set budding more,
And still more, later flowers for the bees,
Until they think the warm days will
never cease;
For Summer has o'er-brimm'd
their clammy cells.

John Keats
Ode to Autumn

FLOWERS

From a golden terrace – amongst the silk cords, the grey gauzes, the verdant velvet and the crystal discs that blacken like bronze in the sun – I see the foxglove open on to a carpet of silver filigrees, of eyes and heads of hair.

Pieces of yellow gold sown on agate, mahogany pillars supporting an emerald dome, bouquets of white satin and delicate ruby canes surround the water rose.

Only such things as a god with enormous blue eyes and formed like snow, the sea and the sky attract the crowd of young and vigorous roses to the marble terraces.

Arthur Rimbaud,
Illuminations

Symbolism/vocabulary of the garden

Herbals were vital sources of information for early gardeners. The Glastonbury Herbal was written during the tenth century. It derives its name from the fact that it was cared for by Glastonbury Abbey for many centuries. Although the text is in Anglo-Saxon, much of it seems to have been directly translated from Greek. Some of the plants in it are referred to only by their Greek names. The whole book was translated into English in 1874 by the Reverend Oswald Cockayne. From it we learn that the Anglo-Saxons knew about grafting. They grafted the cultivated plum on to the native sloe and the pear on to the native *Pyrus domestica*. The peach is also referred to in the Herbal, where it is called the 'Persian apple'. Although some plants are referred to only by their Greek names, but the majority have Saxon ones. What we now categorise as 'herbaceous' plants were called 'worts'. Culinary or medicinal herbs were grown in 'wort beds'

The garden of love

The link between love and the garden can be traced back to the pre-Christian literature of Greece and Rome. Homer's gardens of Alcinous were abundantly fruitful and protected from the reality of changing seasons by a perpetual springtime and a warm west wind. The idea of the garden as a haven from the dangers and worries of the everyday world made it an ideal setting for lovers to meet, and it became a symbol of the harmony and fruitfulness of a loving relationship. Solomon's Song of Songs in the Old Testament of the Bible made another important link between love and the garden. Solomon addresses his wife as 'hortus conclusus, fons signatus, a walled garden and a sealed fountain. The erotic nature of Solomon's poem posed some problems for the Christian world which were resolved by the interpretation of the Song as an allegory of Christ's perfect union with the Church, his bride.

Pea brained?

The form, colour, and taste of various fruits, flowers and vegetables inspire many parallels with human characteristics. We are unlikely to feel sorry for a gooseberry, but we use its name to describe the unfortunate third person who finds him or herself accompanying a romantic couple when three is definitely a crowd. A 'wallflower' is similarly unlucky in love – used to describe a girl, she sits out every dance, clinging to the wall like the flower from which her name derives. To call someone a lemon is to imply that they are a failure or an idiot. You could add insult to injury by calling someone a turnip head or pea brained. A boxer may have a cauliflower ear if he has been hit once too often. To be full of beans implies you are full of energy, while that old chestnut refers to something that has been heard many times before, to the point of boredom. The word 'fruit' itself comes from the Latin word *fructus*, which means to enjoy something. Eve ate the apple in the garden of Eden, and so woman became the forbidden fruit and the child the fruit of her womb.

In Italian, *cogliere qualcuno in castagna*, literally, 'to catch someone with the chestnut', means to catch them red-handed, whereas *andare a ingrassare i cavoli*, or 'going to fatten the cabbages', means to die and be buried, creating fertile soil for the cabbage crop. In German, *kohl haben*, meaning 'to have a cabbage, is the German equivalent of being 'famished'. In Spanish you are turned into mashed potato, *hecho puré*, when you are in a bad way, while in French, *la purée*, or 'mashed potato', means you are penniless. On the other hand, *avoir la frite*, 'to have French fries', is to be excited. If you call someone *une vraie pomme*, 'a real apple', they are a bit of an idiot, but if a Parisian happens to *tomber dans les pommes*, 'fall into the apples', he has vanished. Finally if a Parisian finds himself penniless he is *a la fin des haricots*, 'at the end of the beans,' and wants some money, *il veut son oseille*, 'he wants his sorrel'!

FINALLY, BELOW IS A LIST OF IDIOMS AND EXPRESSIONS THAT INCLUDE FRUIT OR VEGETABLES	
Apples and pears:	stairs (rhyming slang)
Apple pips:	lips (rhyming slang)
Banana factory:	a hectic, horrible or futile situation (US campus slang, 1980s)
Cabbaged:	absolutely exhausted from overwork – i.e. one has become a vegetable (1990s slang)
Veg out:	Slip into completely apathetic state (US campus slang)
Plum job:	excellent job (20th century)
Lettuce:	female genitals, thus shake the lettuce, to urinate (1990s)
Herb:	to rob (1990s, US Black)
Cherry ace:	the face (rhyming slang)
Cherry picker:	large nose, big enough to hang over a branch as a hook while picking cherries from a tree (20th century, US)
Potatoes in the mould:	cold (rhyming slang)
Pear and quince:	a prince (Australia, rhyming slang)
Apricots:	testicles (1990s, Australia)
Grapes:	money (1960s–70s, US Black)
Carrot cruncher:	a visitor to London from the provinces (1960s onwards)

How much do you know?

Test your knowledge by answering the following questions. To check your results, see the answers on page 115 or turn to the relevant chapter.

1) What is Bordeaux mixture?

a - Liquid compost.
b - A copper-sulphate based fungicide.
c - A French planting plan for the vegetable plot.

2) What is a mulch?

a - Organic matter spread over the soil to maintain an even root temperature, suppress weeds and conserve moisture.
b - A type of garden shed often seen in Germany.
c - A hay meadow.

3) What does remontant mean?

a - Badly-drained soil absorbing little of the rainwater that lies on its surface?
b - A cocktail of fertilisers intended for poor soils.
c - A plant that flowers more than once in the same season.

4) What is cutting back?

a - Removing larger branches to make way for new growth.
b - The first mow of the spring.
c - Installing a windbreak to protect delicate shoots.

5) What is grafting?

a - Digging a patch of previously uncultivated ground.
b - Removing the buds from a shrub in flower to encourage growth.
c - A method of propagation by which an artificial union is made between the rootstock of one plant and the scion of another, so that they eventually function as one plant.

6) What does systemic mean?

a - An intensive crop of a single variety.
b - A crop rotation system used in the vegetable garden.
c - A pesticide or fungicide that is absorbed and distributed through a plant when applied to the soil or foliage.

7) What is vermiculite?

a - A harmful insect which tends to infest fruit trees.
b - A fungal growth common on fruit trees.
c - A lightweight mineral often incorporated into potting composts to improve drainage.

8) What is topiary?

a - The art of clipping and training trees and shrubs into various shapes.
b - A network of mole tunnels.
c - A way of plaiting the stems of onions to make a string.

9) Where did the strawberry plant originate?

a - China.
b - Chile.
c - Africa.

10) ...and the melon?
a - Asia.
b - Australia.
c - Central America.

11) Where did the gerbera originate?
a - Europe.
b - Africa.
c - Central Asia.

12) ...and the tulip?
a - Africa.
b - Holland.
c - Persia (Iran).

13) Who was Edward Waller?
a - The person who discovered the first plant hybrid.
b - The gardener who tended the vegetable garden at Hampton Court.
c - The owner and designer of an important 17th-century garden in Buckinghamshire.

14) L. B. Alberti is:
a - The author of l'Alberti, a work on the alchemy of vegetables.
b - The main inventor of the landscaping theories of the Renaissance.
c - A missionary botanist of the 12th century.

15) What does deciduous mean?:
a - Trees, shrubs and plants that lose their foliage in winter.
b - Destructive pests that are impervious to insecticides.
c - Crops that are self-germinating.

16) What is division in the garden?
a - The damage done to tree and shrub branches when split by frost.
b - Dividing the roots of a plant to create several new specimens.
c - Crop propagation in a vegetable garden.

17) Grafting is the cutting of tree branches back to the trunk.
a - True.
b - False.

18) An espaliered plant is pruned into the shape of a lollipop.
a - True.
b - False.

19) A shoot is a stunted cutting.
a - True.
b - False.

20) A succulent is a vegetable with a good flavour and texture.
a - True.
b - False.

21) Germination is disease control in the vegetable garden.
a - True.
b - False.

22) What is horticultural fleece?
a - A man-made, translucent fabric used to protect plants against cold conditions.
b - Leaf growth that is too vigorous, preventing the vegetable producing a crop.
c - An exceptional drought.

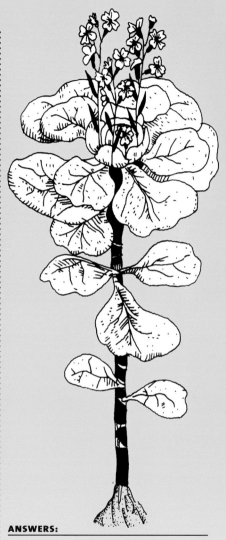

ANSWERS:

1-b; 2-a; 3-c; 4-a; 5-c; 6-c; 7-c; 8-a; 9-b; 10-a; 11-c; 12-c; 13-c; 14-b; 15-a; 16-b; 17-b; 18-b an espaliered plant is trained with the main stem vertical and three or four tiers of branches horizontally on either side; 19-b; a shoot can be a branch, a stem or a twig; 20-b: is a plant with thick, fleshy leaves or stems which are able to store water – such as cacti: 21-b: germination is the first stage of a seed's development into a young plant; 22-a.

Further reading...

General books

The New RHS Encyclopedia of Gardening, Dorling Kindersley.

The RHS Gardeners' Encyclopedia of Plants and Flowers, Dorling Kindersley.

Charlie Dimmock, Enjoy Your Garden: Gardening for Everyone, Michael Joseph.

Vroni Gordon, Shrubs and Trees, Parragon.

The Readers Digest Encyclopedia of Plants and Flowers, Readers Digest.

Alan Titchmarsh, Gardener's World, BBC Books.

Pippa Greenwood, RHS Pests and Diseases, Dorling Kindersley.

Smith and Hawken, William Bryant Logan, The Tool Book, Könemann.

RHS Gardening Manual, Dorling Kindersley.

Richard Bird, Garden Year: Practical Gardening Month by Month, Ward Lock.

David Myers, Best Loved Garden Plants, Parragon.

Will Giles, The New Exotic Garden, Mitchell Beazley.

Beth Chatto, Beth Chatto's Gravel Garden, Frances Lincoln.

Stefan Buczacki, Gardening Britain, BBC Books.

Christopher Lloyd, Christopher Lloyd's Garden Flowers, Cassell & Co.

David Stevens, Garden Design, Conran Octopus.

Elspeth Thompson, The Sunday Telegraph Urban Gardener, Orion.

Sally Court, The Modern Garden Makers, Ward Lock.

Stephen Woodhams, A Portfolio of Contemporary Gardens, Quadrille.

Roy Lancaster, What Perennial Where? Dorling Kindersley.

Stephen Moss, Gardening for Birds, Collins.

Andrew Pfieffer, A Sense of Place, Viking.

Christopher Bradley-Hole, The Minimalist Garden, Mitchell Beazley.

Guy Cooper and Gordon Taylor, Gardens for the Future, Conran Octopus.

HRH The Prince of Wales and Candida Lycett Green, The Garden At Highgrove, Cassell & Co.

Lucy Huntingdon and David Squire, The Garden Colour Directory, Cassell & Co.

Nicola Ferguson, Right Plant, Right Place, Macmillan.

The Oxford Companion to Gardens, OUP.

Monthly and quarterly magazines

The English Garden

BBC Gardener's World

Garden Answers

Gardens Illustrated

Garden Inspirations

The Garden

Hortus

House & Garden

Internet sites

http://www.rhs.org.uk
The Royal Horticultural Society's site, full of advice and information on events, science, education etc, plus a plant finder that covers over 800 UK nurseries.

http://www.grogro.com
Online garden centre run by the Royal Horticultural Society.

http://www.greenfingers.com
A helping hand for all your gardening needs, tips, advice from the experts, shopping and a plant finder.

http://www.myveggiepatch.com
Select a plot to hire and vegetables will be grown on it for you, then delivered fresh to your door on a weekly basis. Plus advice, recipes, shopping.

http://www.treesource.co.uk
For anyone interested in trees. Information on selection and planting, pruning, the law, etc. Also sells books.

http://www.expertgardener.com
An online community that puts you in touch with other gardeners.

http://www.crocus.co.uk
Advice on such things as composting, weathering frost, planting suggestions, plus plant finder and shop.

Parks and gardens

▼

MUSEUM OF GARDEN HISTORY
Lambeth Palace Road,
London SE1 7LB
Tel. 020 7401 8865

CHELSEA PHYSIC GARDEN
66 Royal Hospital Road,
Chelsea,
London SW3 4HS
Tel. 020 7352 5646

CHISWICK HOUSE
Burlington Lane,
Chiswick,
London W4 2RP
Tel. 020 8742 1225

HAM HOUSE
Ham,
Richmond,
Surrey TW10 7RS
Tel. 020 8940 1950

HAMPTON COURT
East Molesey,
Surrey KT8 9AU
Tel. 020 8977 8441

SYON PARK AND GARDENS
Brentford,
Middlesex TW8 8JF
Tel. 020 8560 0881

OSTERLEY PARK HOUSE
Isleworth,
Middlesex TW8 8JF
Tel. 020 8560 3918

FENTON HOUSE
Windmill Hill,
Hampstead,
London NW3 6RT
Tel. 020 7435 3471

SCULPTURE PARKS
Yorkshire Sculpture Garden,
Bretton Hall,
Wakefield,
Yorkshire WF4 4LG
Tel: 01924 830302

FREDERICK GIBBERD'S GARDEN
The House,
Marsh Lane,
Harlow,
Essex CM17 0WA
Tel: 01279 442112

GRIZEDALE FOREST
Hawkshead,
Cumbria

BOTANIC GARDENS

ST ANDREWS BOTANIC GARDEN
Canongate,
St Andrews,
Scotland KY16 8RT
Tel. 01334-477178

ULSTER MUSEUM BOTANIC GARDENS
Belfast,
BT9 5AB
Tel. 028 90 383000

THE ROYAL BOTANIC GARDENS
Kew,
Richmond,
Surrey TW9 3AB
Tel. 020 8940 1171

DUNDEE BOTANIC GARDEN
University of Dundee,
Scotland DD2 1QH
Tel. 01382 566939

HARLOW CARR BOTANICAL GARDENS
Crag Lane,
Harrogate,
North Yorkshire HG3 1QB
Tel. 01423 565418

EDINBURGH ROYAL BOTANIC GARDENS
Inverleith Row,
Edinburgh EH3 5LR
Tel. 031 552 7171

THE NATIONAL BOTANIC GARDEN OF WALES,
Middleton Hall,
Llanarthne,
Carmarthenshire,
Wales SA32 8HG
Tel. 01558 668768

BOTANICAL GARDENS, UNIVERSITY OF CAMBRIDGE
Batemen Street and
Brooklands Avenue,
Cambridge CB2 1JF
Tel. 0223 336265

ROYAL HORTICULTURAL SOCIETY GARDENS
Hyde Hall,
Rettendon,
Chelmsford,
Essex CM3 8ET
Tel. 01245 400256

ROSEMOOR
Great Torrington,
Devon EX38 8PH
Tel. 01805 624067

WISLEY
Woking,
Surrey, GU23 6QB
Tel. 01483 224234

ANTRIM CASTLE GARDENS
Randalstown Road,
Antrim,
County Antrim,
BT41 4LH,
Northern Ireland
Tel. 028 9446 0360

HILLSBOROUGH CASTLE GARDEN
The Square,
Hillsborough,
Co. Down, BT26 6HG
Northern Ireland

ARBORETA

BEDGEBURY
The National Pinetum,
Goudhurst,
Cranbrook,
Kent,
TN17 2SL
Tel. 01580 211044

BLUEBELL ARBORETUM AND NURSERY
Annwell Lane,
Smisby,
Ashby-de-la-Zouch,
LE65 2TA
Tel. 01530 413700

BROGDALE HORTICULTURAL TRUST
Brogdale Road,
Faversham,
Kent, ME13 8XZ
Tel. 01795 535286

WESTONBIRT ARBORETUM
3 miles SW of Tetbury on
the A433 Bath Road,
20 minutes NE of M4
junctions 18 and 20
Gloucestershire, GL8 8QS
Tel 01666 880220

DERBY ARBORETUM

Arboretum Square,
Derby DE23 8FN
Tel. 01332 716644

THE QUINTA ARBORETUM

Swettenham Village,
nr Congleton,
Cheshire, CW12 2LD
Tel. 01270 610180

SIR HAROLD HILLIER GARDENS AND ARBORETUM

Jermyns Lane,
Ampfield,
Romsey,
Hampshire, SO51 0QA
Tel. 01794 368787

OTHER GARDENS OPEN TO THE PUBLIC

BARRINGTON COURT

Garden designed by
Gertrude Jekyll, consisting of
a series of 'walled rooms',
including the White
Garden, the Rose and Iris
Gardens, and the Lily
Garden. Vegetable garden
with espalier-trained fruit
trees, cider apple orchard
and a profusion of clematis,
wisteria and honeysuckle.
Near Ilminster, Somerset
Tel. 01460 241938

BIDDULPH GRANGE GARDEN

A rare example of a garden
straight from the great
Victorian era. A series of
connected 'compartments'
consisting of an Egyptian
palace, a Chinese pagoda...
A tour of the world of
gardens in miniature
Biddulph,
near Stoke-on-Trent,
Staffordshire, ST8 7SD
Tel. 01782 517999

BODNANT GARDEN

One of the most beautiful
gardens in Wales.
Splendid collections of
rhododendrons, magnolias,
camellias; nineteenth-
century, formal terraced
gardens. Laburnum tunnel.
Tal-y-Cafn,
Colwyn Bay,
Clwyd, LL28 5RE
Tel. 01492 650640

BRANKLYN GARDEN

Remarkable gardens of
considerable botanical
interest. Splendid collection
of dwarf rhododendrons.
Perth,
Tayside
Tel. 01738 625535

BRESSINGHAM GARDENS

English garden measuring 2
hectares (5 acres) containing
5,000 species of perennial
plants and alpines.
Near Diss,
Norfolk
Tel. 01379 687386

CAWDOR CASTLE

Possibly the most romantic
castle in the Highlands of
Scotland. Classical garden,
walled garden, holly maze.
Cawdor,
Nairn, Highlands,
Scotland
Tel. 01667 404615

CHATSWORTH

One of the most grandiose
stately homes in England,
surrounded by a
landscaped park designed
by Capability Brown, with
sophisticated cascades and
fountains. Yew maze.
Bakewell,
Derbyshire
Tel. 01246 582204

DRUMMOND CASTLE GARDENS

Extraordinary garden laid
out in parterres with a very
complex classical design,
situated on a wooded
hillside and dominated by a
castle.
Near Criff,
Tayside
Tel. 01764 681321

EDZELL CASTLE

The most ancient surviving
walled garden in Great
Britain.
Edzell,
near Brechin,
Tayside
Tel. 01356 648631

ERDDIG

A rare example of a
traditional eighteenth-
century garden, lovingly
restored. A large walled
garden containing varieties
of fruit trees which were
cultivated during that
period.
Near Wrexham,
Clwyd
Tel. 01987 313333

GARDENS OF THE ROSE

Specialised gardens of the
Royal National Rose Society
containing 30,000 roses.
Chiswell Green,
St. Albans,
Hertfordshire
Tel. 01727 850461

HAMPTON COURT PALACE

Henry VIII's palace built on
the banks of the Thames,
surrounded by a wild
garden, a knot garden, and
rose garden as well as the
famous maze and the Great
Vine planted in 1768.
East Molesey,
Surrey
Tel. 01817 819500

HELIGAN GARDENS

The site of the greatest
project in horticultural
restoration in Europe,
undertaken in 1991. Rock
gardens, summer pavilions,
a crystal grotto, an
Italianate garden, a magic
well, walled gardens; a
subtropical valley
dominating the picturesque
fishing village of
Mevagissey.
Pentewan,
St Austell, Cornwall
Tel. 01726 844157

INVEREWE GARDEN

Remarkable garden in the
Highlands situated in an
impressive mountainous
landscape on the shores of
Loch Ewe.
Plants from all over the
world.
Poolewe,
near Gairloch,
Highlands,
Scotland
Tel. 01445 781200

COLETON FISHACRE GARDEN

Garden designed by Lady
Dorothy d'Oyly Carte in a
small sheltered valley. Large
variety of rare trees and
exotic plants.
Near Kingswear,
Devon
Tel. 01803 752466

THREAVE GARDEN & ESTATE

Large gardens, greenhouses,
vegetable gardens, peat and
rock gardens. The 200
varieties of daffodils are a
delight in spring.
Near Castle Douglas,
Dumfries & Galloway,
Scotland
Tel. 01556 502575

TREBAH GARDEN
*Rhododendrons more than
100 years old and
subtropical glades with tree
ferns.
Near Falmouth,
Cornwall*
Tel. 01326 250448

SISSINGHURST GARDEN
*This is the most famous
20th century garden in
England and a fine
example of the Arts and
Crafts style. Designed in
part by Harold Nicolson in
the 1930s, his wife, Vita
Sackville-West was
responsible for the artistic
planting layout.
Sissinghurst
Cranbrook
Kent, TN17 2AB*
Tel. 01580 715330

HIDCOTE MANOR GARDEN
*Designed and laid out by
Lawrence Johnston over a
period of 40 years from
around 1907, this famous
garden displays an
interesting sequence of
garden rooms, each with
their own special character.
Chipping Camden
Gloucestershire, GL55 6LR*
Tel. 01386 438333

STOURHEAD
*Created by a wealthy
English banker with a
passion for art, this garden
design pays tribute to the
great landscape painters of
the 17th century.
Near Warminster
Wiltshire, BA12 6QD*
Tel. 01747 841152

SCHOOLS, TRAINING, DEVELOPMENT

THE SOCIETY OF GARDEN DESIGNERS
*The Institute of
Horticulture,
14/15 Belgrave Square,
London SW1X 8PS*
Tel. 020 7 838 9311

THE ROYAL HORTICULTURAL SOCIETY
*80 Vincent Square,
London SW1P 2PE*
Tel. 020 7834 4333

ASSOCIATION OF PROFESSIONAL LANDSCAPERS
*Creighton Lodge,
Hollington Lane,
Stramshall, Uttoxeter*
Tel. 01889 507256

THE ENGLISH GARDENING SCHOOL
*66 Hospital Road,
London SW3 4HS*
Tel. 020 7352 4347

CAPEL MANOR COLLEGE
*Bullsmore Lane,
Enfield,
Middlesex EN1 4RQ*
Tel. 020 8366 4442

PICKARD SCHOOL OF GARDEN DESIGN
*16 Stafford Street,
Ecclerhall,
Staffordshire*
Tel. 01785 859179

MERRIST WOOD COLLEGE
*Worplesdon,
Guildford,
Surrey*
Tel. 01483 884040

European Gardens

FRANCE

PARC ANDRÉ CITROËN
*métro Balard,
75015 Paris*

DÉSERT DE RETZ
*allée Frédéric-Passy,
78240 Chambourcy*

PARC DU CHÂTEAU DE COURANCES
01490 Milly-la-Forêt

PARC DU CHÂTEAU DE COURSON
91680 Courson-Monteloup
Tel. 0033 64 58 90 12
coursondom@aol.com

JARDINS CLAUDE MONET
*Les Jardins de Giverny,
27620 Giverny.*
Tel. 0033 32 71 05 80
www.fondation-monet.com

JARDIN DE CHATEAUBRIAND
*La Vallée aux Loups,
Maison de Chateaubriand,
87, rue de Chateaubriand,
92290 Châtenay-Malabry*
Tel. 0033 47 02 08 62
www.terresdecrivains.com

PARC DE BAGATELLE, BOIS DE BOULOGNE
*Route de Sèvres-Neuilly,
75016 Paris*
Tel. 0033 40 71 75

JARDINS DU CHÂTEAU DE VILLANDRY
37510 Villandry
Tel. 0033 47 50 02 09
villandry@wanadoo.fr

SPAIN

L'ALHAMBRA AND THE GENERALIFE
*The sumptuous gardens of
the Generalife stretch
beyond the main entrance
of the Alhambra Palace and
shelter canals, fountains
and fountain jets.
Grenada*
Tel. 0034 958 22 09 12

RETIRO PARK AND BOTANICAL GARDENS
*Retiro Park is a green oasis,
right in the heart of
Madrid. The botanical
gardens are situated on the
other side of Alfonso-XIII
avenue. Trees, shrubs,
flowers collected from
around the world.
Madrid.*

THE ALCAZAR, SEVILLE
*The Alcazar palace was
constructed in the ninth
century. Dating from the
Moorish era, only these
marvellous gardens have
survived.
Plaza Triunfo, 41001 Seville.*
Tel. 00 34 95 422 71 63

PARC GÜELL
*The city-garden conceived
by Gaudi.
Barcelona.*
http://titan.iwu.edu-
cferrada/spa315

BOTANICAL GARDENS
Designed in 1795, the garden contains no less than 1,500 tropical species. Tenerife, Carretera Botanico, 38400 Puerto de la Cruz

THE ALCAZAR, CORDOBA
Behind the palace walls, constructed by the Catholic monarchs, stretches a sophisticated garden with flower parterres, palms and countless fountains.
Calle Caballerizas Reales, 14002 Cordoba
Tel. 0034 957 42 01 51

HUERTO DEL CURA
The Huerto del Cura (the priest's orchard) houses the most important palm grove in Europe.
Huerto de Cura, 03203 Elche
Tel. 0034 965 45 96 67

PALACIO DE VIANA
Open every day except Wednesdays. The charm of a house surrounded by 13 terraces with fountains, flowering pot plants. Citrus fruits, agaves.
Piazza de Don Gome, Cordoba
Tel. 0034 957 48 22 75

ITALY
For more information contact: Great Italian Gardens, Piazza Cavour, 622060 Cabiate (Como).
Tel. 0039 0756 211
Fax: 0039 0756 768
www.thais.it/itinerati/gran digiardini

VILLA GRABAU
A nine-hectare (22-acre) park with a garden in the English style, rare botanical specimens, palm collection

and Italian Renaissance gardens with terraces.
Via Matraia 29 San Pancrazio, 55010 Saltocchio, Tuscany
Tel./fax: 0039 0583 406 098

CORSINI GARDENS
Italian Renaissance garden designed by Bernardo Buontalenti in 1572.
Via Il Prato, 58 50123 Florence, Tuscany
Tel. 0039 055 218 994

VILLA ARVEDI
A villa garden in an extraordinarily well preserved condition. Displays all the characteristics typical of a Venetian garden in the seventeenth century.
37023, Grezzana, Verona, Veneto
Tel. 0039 045 907 045

VILLA CICOGNA MOZZONI
Formal Italian garden with terraces, secret garden, water staircase and a romantic park.
Piazza Cicogna 8, 21050 Bisuschio (Varese), Lombardy.
Tel. 0039 0332 471 134

VILLA BORGHESE
A vast English style park created in the 17th century full of trees, lakes and villas. Top of via Vittorio Veneto, near Porta Pinciana, Rome

VILLA CELIMONTANA GARDENS
A charming park of trees and shrubs near the Celian Hill.
Piazza della Navicella, Rome

ORTO BOTANICO
Rome's Botanical Gardens located in the Trastevere district. A peaceful and romantic place in the heart of the city, it is frequented more by locals than by tourists.
Largo Cristina di Svezia, 24
Tel. 0039 066 864 193

VILLA MEDICI GIULINI
The sixteenth century garden of the Villa Medici is one of the most ancient in Lombardy.
Via Medici 6, 20040 Briosco, Milan
Tel. 0039 0362 958 165

VILLA MARIGOLA
Viale Biagini, San Terenzo Lerici (La Spezia).
Garden on a promontory dominating the Golfo dei Poeti.
Tel. 0039 0187 773 318

PALAZZO FANTINI
Tredozio, Forlì.
Italian garden, large collection of aromatic plants, museum of agricultural implements.
Tel. 0039 051 330 095

PALAZZO GRIFONI BUDINI GATTAJ
Piazza SS Anunziata 1, 50122 Florence, Tuscany.
A romantic garden.
Tel. 0039 055 210 832

SWITZERLAND

VILLA FAVORITA
Terraces, avenues of exotic species.
Castagnola, Lugano, Switzerland.
Tel. 0041 91 9721 741

GERMANY

BOTANISCHER GARDEN UND BOTANISCHES MUSEUM BERLIN-DAHLEM (BGBM)
The Botanic Garden in Berlin is over 300 years old and is one of the world's largest and most important gardens covering an area of 126 acres with over 20,000 different species of plants.
Freie Universität Berlin
Königin-Luise-Str 6-8
14191 Berlin
Tel 0049 30 838 50100
Info. 0049 30 838 50027

ENGLISCHERGARTEN MÜNCHEN
Created by Lüdwig von Schell and Count Rumford, this garden was one of the first European parks designed for public use.
80805 München
Tel. 0049 89 335169

PALMENGARTEN
The Palmengarten in Frankfurt is renowned throughout the world for its collection of tropical plants. It has one of the largest greenhouse complexes in the world, the Tropicarium which covers 500 m2.
Siesmayerstrasse 61
D-60323 Frankfurt am Main
Tel. 0049 69 212
33939/36689

SCHWETZINGER SCHLOSSGARTEN
Based on the gardens at Versailles, the Schwetzinger Palace Gardens consist of a French baroque garden and an English landscape garden. It was designed by JL Petri in 1753.
Schwetzinen
Baden-Würtemburg
Tel. 0049 06 202 81481

ACID

Soil with a PH value of less than 7.

AERATE

Loosen compacted soil to allow air to enter.

ALKALINE

Soil with a PH value of more than 7.

ANNUAL

A plant that completes its growing cycle in one season.

BAREROOT

A plant supplied without any growing medium around its roots.

BIENNIAL

A plant that completes its life cycle over a period of two years.

BLANCH

Exclude light from developing leaves and stems to encourage tender growth in vegetables.

CLIMBER

A plant that climbs using other plants or structures as support.

COLLAR

The part of the plant where the roots meet the stem, also known as the 'neck'.

COMPOST

Organic material, rich in humus, formed by the decomposed remains of plants and other organic waste.

CONIFER

Evergreen trees and shrubs, often bearing cones.

CUTTINGS

A portion of a plant (a leaf, shoot, root or bud) that is cut off to be used for propagation.

DEAD HEADING

Cutting off the spent flowers of shrubs, annuals and perennials.

DECIDUOUS

Plants that shed leaves at the end of the growing season.

EARTHING UP

Drawing the earth up around the stems of plants to protect from the cold.

ESPALIER

Method of training trees and shrubs, particularly fruit trees, with a central, vertical stem and three or more layers of horizontal branches.

FERTILISER

A variety of substances, including manure, compost and dried blood, added to the soil to increase its fertility, thus improving the level of nutrients available to plants.

FESCUES

Grass species

FUNGICIDE

A chemical that kills fungi, particularly those responsible for plant diseases.

GRAFTING

A method of propagation by which an unnatural union is made between the scion of one plant and the rootstock of another.

GRAFTING TAPE OR WAX

Tape or wax used to protect the graft union during healing.

GREEN MANURE

A quick maturing, leafy crop, grown specifically to be dug back into the soil.

HORTICULTURAL FLEECE

A man-made, translucent fabric used to protect plants against cold conditions.

HUMUS

The organic residue of decayed vegetable matter in the soil.

LATERALS

A side growth arising from a shoot or root.

LAYERING

A method of propagation by which a shoot is encouraged to produce roots while still attached to the parent plant.

LEAF MOULD

Fallen leaves rotted down to be used as a soil improver.

MANURE

Animal dung used to mulch and enrich soil.

MULCH

Material applied to the surface of the soil to suppress weeds, conserve moisture and improve soil structure.

NODE

The point on a stem from which leaves, shoots or branches grow

NUTRIENTS

Minerals used by plants to promote growth.

PEAT

Partly decayed, humus-rich vegetation formed on the surface of waterlogged soils.

PERENNIALS

Any plant that lives for three seasons or more.

PERLITE

Small granules of volcanic material that are added to compost to improve aeration and drainage.

PERPETUAL

Repeat fruiting.

PH

A measure of acidity or alkalinity of soil.

PINCH OUT

Removal of the growing tip of the plant to encourage the growth of side shoots.

POTTING COMPOST

A mixture of loam, peat substitutes, sand and nutrients, in varying proportions.

PRICK OUT

Transplanting of young seedlings to give them room to grow.

PROPAGATION

The increase of plants using seeds or other, vegetative, methods.

PRUNING

Trimming or cutting back a plant to encourage healthy, shapely growth, flowering and/or fruiting.

REMONTANT

A plant that flowers more than once a season.

ROOT BALL

The roots and accompanying soil visible when a plant is dug up.

ROOTSTOCK

A plant used to provide the root system for a grafted plant.

RUNNER

Seedling strawberry plant, still attached to parent plant by long, running stem.

Glossary

SCARIFY

For lawns, to remove moss and dead growth from the lawn, using a scarifier or a rake.
For seed, abrasion of the outer coat of the seed to improve water intake and speed up germination.

SCION

A shoot or bud cut from one plant to graft on to a rootstock.

SEED TRAYS

A shallow wooden or plastic tray used for germinating seeds and growing seedlings on after pricking out.

SEMI-RIPE CUTTING

A cutting taken from semi-mature wood during the growing season.

SHRUB

A woody stemmed plant without a single trunk.

SPECIES

In plant classification, the species is the principal rank below genus, containing closely related, very similar plants.

SUBSOIL

Layers of soil beneath the topsoil that are generally less fertile than the topsoil.

SUCKER

A shoot that rises from the plant's underground stem or roots.

SYSTEMIC

A pesticide or fungicide that is absorbed and distributed through the plant.

THINNING OUT

Removal of surplus branches to allow light into the heart of the plant.

TOPIARY

Training small-leaved trees and shrubs into various shapes

TOPSOIL

The top layer of soil, which is usually fertile.

TUBER

An underground organ, developed from the stem, which is used for food storage.

VARIETY

In botanical terms, a naturally occurring variant of a wild species.

VERMICULITE

A mica-like mineral that is added to soil to improve the aeration and drainage.

'God Almighty first planted a garden;
and, indeed, it is the purest of human pleasures'.

Francis Bacon,
1561–1626

Contents

Fact ⟫ 2–12
Fun facts and quick quotes

Discover ⟫ 13–38

Look ⟫ 39–58
At work and at play on allotments

In practice ⟫ 59–96

Find out ⟫ 97–125

Credits